Fundamentals of Apostolic Leadership

D. Dean Anderson, Ed.D.

ISBN- 9781089023883

Praise for *Fundamentals of Apostolic Leadership*

"The church needs leaders with a clear direction for how to approach the future. Leadership comes down to taking ownership of the challenges that come. Dr. Dean Anderson has provided an inspirational and informative work for those of us called to lead the body of Christ in these changing times. The principles presented here will better equip us to lead as we head out into the great unknown."
- C. Myles Young

"If you are wrestling with leadership in your church, are looking to further the mission of the church or would like to develop your or your saints' leadership skills, then this book is for you. Bro. Dean Anderson has been involved in ministry and in leadership of the highest level. His insight into the topic of leadership, and particularly leadership in the church, will identify areas that need work in your life while providing clear, concise methods to address them in top-notch fashion. You will be blessed after reading this book!"
- Nathaniel Urshan

"Most leadership books tend to lean heavily on principle, neglecting practical application entirely, or they're full of tools, but lack grounding in biblical foundation. *Fundamentals of Apostolic Leadership* thoroughly addresses both the practical and the principle, and is complete with examples from a diverse array of apostolic ministerial contexts. As a mental health professional, it's refreshing to see communication and conflict resolution skills unpacked in such an accessible way. The Apostolic movement is blessed to have this resource available to educate and equip."
- Karissa King

Dedication

This book is dedicated to the three most influential leaders in my life: Robert Geans, Sr., C. Myles Young and Nathaniel J. Wilson.

No one has contributed more to my development as the leader of my home than Robert Geans, Sr. My time spent under his ministry was formative and foundational. Thank you, Sir, for your investment into my family.

C. Myles Young has inspired me on a level unparalleled by any other leader. Your vision for global reach and revival constantly challenges me to do more for the Kingdom of God.

Bishop Nathaniel J. Wilson believed in me and provided an opportunity for world class development as a leader. I am most blessed to have a close relationship with this hero of the faith.

Contents

Acknowledgements

I want to thank my three children for their diligent efforts in the editing and formatting of this book. Brett meticulously perused the front material for proper format and consistency. Danielle provided cover design by aligning fonts, color schemes and appropriate spacing. Kara served as primary editor, painstakingly examining every word and phrase ensuring proper grammar, syntax and structure.

I would also like to thank my loving wife, Karen, for her unending support. I love doing life with you.

This book would not be possible without my precious family. Thank you for helping me realize this dream. I love you.

Foreword

While there are many leadership books in the world, there are few that begin the quest for individual actualization at the foundation of human leadership, that is, the human spirit. It is here that both author and reader must intersect before the foray into empowerment and enablement can become deep, robust, and authentically great. Dr. Dean Anderson here provides numerous solid and cogent insights into the far-ranging subject of leadership.

In the infinite reposes the ideal self of each of us as we are when actualized into the exact image of God as originally designed. Discipleship consists of movement, sometimes rapidly, sometimes very incrementally, toward this goal. This is "growing in grace" and "becoming." The life of Dr. Anderson over the last decade is a personal model of what occurs when an individual finds the path to personal actualization and follows it in the Holy Ghost. His recognizing the open door, and continuing obedience in refusing to deviate therefrom, has led him to blessing and a flourishing which would otherwise never have occurred. In turn, this outflow of new open doors has overflowed to his entire family, who are blessed because of his ongoing compliance to his personal, God-ordained, destiny.

Reading the book while knowing these things about the author reinforces every important leadership discussion contained in the book.

May you, the reader, be richer for the reading.

~ Nathaniel J. Wilson

Chapter One

The Importance of Leadership

It could be argued that nothing is more critical to the success of any organization than its leadership. While many factors naturally coalesce to produce desired results and accomplish the mission of an institution, without solid leadership the likelihood of success drops significantly. This reality is no respecter of organizations as it is true in institutions of learning, non-profits, businesses and even spiritual enterprises.

Inherent in human nature is the desire to be led. Looking to leaders for direction, stability, strength and predictability gives a sense of security to members of the organization. This truth has spawned an enormous market for leadership literature. Countless books have been written about characteristics of leadership. Additionally, numerous biographies of famous leaders have been published. These books often propose to present the distilled essence of what makes an effective leader. Many of these works have value and present concepts and practices that enhance one's understanding and ability to lead. Some are particularly helpful in presenting the fundamentals of leadership.

Many books have also been published about church leadership. There are admittedly universal facets of leadership. There are also characteristics of leadership that are more relevant to spiritual leadership in general, and to Apostolic leadership specifically. The intention of this book is to present components of leadership that are necessary for effective Apostolic leadership.

Leading in specific industries entails unique dynamics necessary for success. For example, when leading a sales team, the art of initial contact, negotiation and closing the deal are critical techniques to convey to the team. In a situation like this, the end game is profit. It is incumbent upon leadership to transfer an understanding of the theory and practice of these concepts. In the work of God, the responsibility of the leader is to inspire others to fulfill the mandate of the church.

The two pillars upon which the mission of the church rests are evangelism and discipleship. The church exists to reach the lost and perfect the saints. Essentially, our role is to lead people to salvation and help keep them saved. It is possible for a local church to be much stronger in one area than

2

the other. This creates an imbalance and inhibits overall effectiveness. For some pastors, reaching the lost at any cost is the ultimate goal. While the importance of this cannot be overemphasized, exclusive focus on evangelism neglects the necessary component of development of the saints. What good is a 100 soul revival if none of them are discipled and become solid members of the church? Likewise, if a church never reaches for the lost, but focuses entirely on member development, eventually the church will cease to exist. A balance is needed in which evangelism results in converts who are appropriately grounded in truth.

Accomplishing this critical balance requires effective leadership. Some pastors and leaders are more naturally inclined to soul-winning rather than teaching. Other leaders are more adept at teaching, but not as effective in witnessing. Wise leaders will surround themselves with others who possess qualities they do not. A charismatic "people person" who has never met a stranger and for whom sharing their faith comes easily may be effective in leading others in how to engage in communication with potential converts. However, teaching doctrine and grounding new converts in the faith may not be one of their strengths. In this case, the overall goals of the church are better served when this leader employs others to address the areas in which he or she is lacking.

The good news is that there is ample room for many to be used in leadership. A local congregation has one pastor and perhaps a bishop. However, there may be several lay leaders whose roles are critical to the overall success of the church. The Scripture teaches, "And he gave some apostles; and some prophets; and some evangelists; and some pastors and teachers; for the perfecting of the saints, for the work of the ministry, for the edifying of the body of Christ" (Ephesians 4:11-12). The Bible also mentions "helps" (I Corinthians 12:28). This comes from a Greek word that is very rare in Scripture, only appearing twice. It refers to the grace and power of God to meet one's need specifically through a person whom the Lord directs. This type of person is inherently a leader. Exerting influence, meeting needs and strengthening someone's faith are results of leadership.

Church leadership can take on many forms. Not everyone is called to a pulpit ministry or a pastorate. There are many other ways in which the church is edified. Some are effective as Sunday school teachers or bus workers. Others are gifted in teaching Bible studies or witnessing to the lost. There are also those whose strengths lie more in hospitality and service. Leaders must be able to determine both the gifts and passions of saints to appropriately maximize their potential for service. This is not only rewarding for the one ministering, but is also beneficial in contributing to the overall success of the church.

Identifying and utilizing specific talents and passions of saints is not always an easy task. It is helpful to provide venues through which people are given the opportunity to shine. Certain individuals may have a natural giftedness in an area about which they are not passionate. Others may have a desire for a particular ministry in which they are not particularly adept. This is not to advocate the idea that one must be talented to be used. Passion is a powerful driving force. Even if someone lacks initial aptitude, strong desire to work in area will often produce skill over time. It is typically a best practice to utilize a less gifted saint in an area of passion rather than a talented saint with little passion for the job. Disinterest is easily identified and will create negative energy in a department.

You may wonder how passions can be identified. One large Apostolic church initiated a program entitled Passion-Based Ministries. Much like the name suggests, the idea was to allow members to approach a committee with ministry ideas in areas of specific interest to them. This allowed ministries to develop organically as opposed to creating a ministry and then looking for someone to fill the role as leader. Certain criteria were developed to set parameters ensuring any suggested idea would fit the overall mission of the church. Inevitably, some proposals were submitted which were self-serving and not congruent with the church's vision. In these cases, the committee reviewed the proposal and took appropriate action regarding approval.

The idea of passion-based ministries proved successful, as it activated both creativity and passion in the saints. One sister developed a quilting ministry with other saints. Their purpose was to sew quilts for saints who had been ill. This presented a meaningful token of the love of the church in someone's time of need. This also provided a physical gift that would serve as a reminder and connection to the church. Such a ministry fit the spirit of passion-based ministries.

Another example is found in a ministry that arose known as Boys' Club. This was led by a former college basketball player who possessed a desire to help boys and young men engage in healthy activities that would promote unity as well as allegiance to the church. Vision for this ministry included teaching teamwork, respect, cooperation and handling defeat. The young men would compete in various sports including basketball, football and softball. This continued for several years as a successful ministry promoting healthy fellowship for young men as they developed into mature Christians. An additional benefit was that many of the young men developed lasting and meaningful relationships with their coaches, which resulted in mentorships.

Many other passion-based ministries could be cited that strengthened the church through concerted efforts which met the needs of saints. The principle is that leadership is needed in multiple areas of the church. Regardless of the level of leadership, certain fundamentals are necessary in order for leadership to be effective.

Chapter Two

On Being a Leader

When the subject of leadership is broached, various ideas may be conjured up. Some may focus on readily identifiable characteristics of leadership such as sound judgment and impartiality. Others may think about world figures such as heads of state or other politicians. Still others may think of leaders of particular organizations such as businesses, sports teams or the military. John Wooden, Dwight D. Eisenhower or Jack Welch might come to mind due to their exceptional success in their respective fields. For Apostolics, perhaps giants of the faith who have gone before us would be our first inclination.

While there would be no incorrect response, an in-depth examination of leadership would probably need to start with at least a general definition of leadership. One of the foremost experts on leadership, particularly in Christian circles, distilled leadership down to a single word: influence (Maxwell, 2012). This may oversimply such a grandiose topic, but essentially all leadership inherently includes this by definition or it would not be leadership. If a leader does not influence others, how is he or she leading?

One thing to keep in mind when discussing leadership is the fact that many times the context determines the proper approach. For example, one could study types of leadership such as autocratic, laissez-faire, transactional, democratic, transformational, etc. and find valid points in all of them. However, this does not mean that any one style is best for every situation. There is not a one-size-fits-all element in leadership. Many examples could be cited to validate that the best leadership style is often situational.

In the military, for example, an autocratic leadership style is necessary. It is not difficult to imagine the disastrous results if commanding officers used a democratic approach and allowed subordinates to collectively determine decisions. Even worse consequences would ensue if a laissez-faire style were utilized in which individuals were allowed to make specific decisions personally. By contrast, this hands-off approach has proven exceptionally successful in certain multibillion-dollar companies such as Google.

A laissez-faire style leadership has served Google well as they have traditionally hired talented engineers and allowed them to work essentially uninhibited. The creativity this fostered produced one of the leading tech companies in America. If these creative geniuses would have been micromanaged, there is little doubt that the innovation that literally changed the world in many ways would not have transpired.

Recently, observations by executives in Google's human resources department prompted a thorough examination of primary traits of its most effective leaders. A senior executive observed, "Our best managers have teams that perform better, are retained better, are happier—they do everything better. So the biggest controllable factor that we could see was the quality of the manager, and how they sort of made things happen. The question we then asked was, what if every manager was that good?" (Bryant, 2011). The pursuit of answering this question birthed a project acquiring considerable qualitative and quantitative data. This venture concluded with a list of eight consistent qualities found in successful managers (Bryant, 2011). The list contained some surprises, as traits once considered most necessary were significantly outranked by more personal attributes. Technical expertise in a leader was far outpaced by willingness to engage one-on-one. The top eight most desirable traits were as follows:

1. Be a good coach.
2. Empower your team but don't micromanage.
3. Express interest in your team members' success and well-being.
4. Be productive and results-oriented.
5. Be a good communicator and listen to your team.
6. Help your employees with career development.
7. Have a clear vision and strategy for the team.
8. Have technical skills so you can advise them.

This list provides insight into the needs of subordinates which can enhance a leader's effectiveness. Some of these are obviously more applicable to Apostolic leadership than others. When considered as a whole, utilizing these tactics certainly contributes to desired results. The caveat for Apostolic leaders is that we are not simply managers. The preceding list focuses more on management than leadership. Relevant to this discussion is the difference between managers and leaders.

While both are necessary even in the church, those who provide ultimate leadership are the visionaries who present the grand dream. Such people fall much more into the leader category rather than the manager category. Leaders cast vision and give an overall image of the mission. A manager's primary responsibility is to carry out the logistics of the operation. The main focus in our discussion is how we can maximize our potential as Apostolic leaders. This includes leadership roles in the church as well as being leaders in our everyday lives.

One fundamental understanding that is crucial in Apostolic leadership is the fact that we are leaders at all times. Leadership is not a hat we put on when addressing a group in a department head meeting. It is not something that can be turned on and off depending on the circumstances. In other words, authentic leadership is not part time. You might be a part time manager on your job. When your shift is over you can take off the uniform and not worry about company rules. If you are the owner of the company, however, your concern is present at all times. When you are a leader, it is not a position, it's a lifestyle.

This is not to imply that everyone squarely falls into one category or the other. There is obviously overlap to some degree, but there are notable differences. Managers primarily concern themselves with process and function. They manage workflow by making sure rules are observed, deadlines are met and so forth. Ultimately their goals are quantifiable based on metrics. An effective manager will have accomplished X this month, Y the next month and be appropriately compensated. Theirs is a world that can be measured. Management is more about counting value than creating value. Management is concerned with giving instructions, which most often are prescribed. Managers give directives such as fill this bin, send this package, count this pallet of inventory. There is nothing particularly inspirational in such directives.

Leadership, by contrast, goes to the level of inspiration. It is much more qualitative, and therefore, its influence is not as easily quantifiable. Leadership is about invoking an emotional state which ideally results in followers internalizing the mission. Rather than following rules just for the sake of compliance, followers then catch the spirit of the mission and personalize it. The synergy this creates maximizes operational success. People are going to follow leaders more for who they are rather than for the institution or position they represent.

This brings us to the idea of positional leadership versus relational leadership. As the name implies, positional leadership is based on the office one holds. Subordinates may be deferential because of obligation or respect for the position of a leader. For example, a boss may come up with a terribly flawed idea. Depending on the demeanor of this individual, subordinates may not point out the obvious deficiencies in the proposal for fear of retribution or public chastisement. In cases like this, the lack of healthy discussion necessary for determining a viable proposal is most likely not due to superior intelligence in the leader, but rather due to intimidation. Positional leadership gives the one in charge the authority to make decisions. However, sincere respect for the leader's competency may not exist in subordinates.

In contrast to positional leadership is relational leadership. Anyone can possess relational leadership because it is not based on office, but rather on actions. Relational leadership engenders trust and respect from others. What is unique about this type of leadership is that one can possess it at any level in an organization. This is not reserved for people in authority. Relational leadership accrues power organically through interactions between people. In these exchanges, genuine love and concern is felt, creating a bond that supersedes roles.

Worthy of note is the fact that positional leadership and relational leadership are not mutually exclusive. It is entirely possible to possess both, and many people do. In any leadership context, an exceptional leader may have both positional and relational leadership. It is also true that one does not necessitate the other. It is sometimes easier to identify those who only have positional leadership. This is the case because of the common assumption that authentic leaders should not possess apparent flaws. In the spotlight of leadership, sometimes deficiencies are more easily noticed.

In an Apostolic context, it is not difficult to determine which type of leadership is most effective. Being a relational leader finds its roots theologically in Scripture and builds camaraderie and unity amongst the body. Positions are necessary and often biblical; however, striving for a leadership role for the sake of the spotlight and presumed prestige reveals damaging ulterior motives. Most of us are familiar with leaders who have been adamant about proclaiming their position or authority. The reality is that the more a leader has to remind people of his or her authority, the less real authority is possessed.

It is possible to effectively accomplish nothing through positional leadership alone. Just because someone is given a title does not mean that he or she knows how to utilize resources to accomplish tasks. Unfortunately, incompetence exists in leadership as in other areas of life. It could also be argued that it is difficult to accomplish nothing with relational leadership. The reason is that when respect for an individual is present, others are more willing to sacrifice and rally as a team to accomplish a mission. This is the epitome of influence.

As Apostolic leaders, we work to build relationships and not to seek titles. Our good example of faithfulness, obedience, kindness and other leadership qualities will inevitably have an effect on those around us. This will breed respect and willing cooperation. Naturally, working with people who desire to cooperate is much preferred to working with those who need persuasion or coercion to get on board. The former group typically only needs general direction.

Leadership is more about general guidance than explicit commands. There is an element of giving directives, but these are not necessarily specific. An example might be that a worker is told to be at a certain location at 3 o'clock to pick up a product. This person needs to calculate the best route, resources, etc. to make this happen. He must account for traffic, construction and any other potential obstacles and adjust plans accordingly. He was told what to do, but not exactly how to do it. He was not given a map, but a guideline.

A biblical example of this principle can be found in II Kings chapter 13. In this setting, the prophet Elisha had become sick unto death. King Joash visited the aged prophet lamenting his imminent departure. In final instructions regarding Syrian oppression, the prophet commanded Joash to smite the ground with arrows. The king's response was to smite the ground three times. The prophet became upset with the king and prophesied the ensuing result of his actions. The casual observer might wonder what the king did wrong. He was technically obedient to the command of the prophet. What he did not realize was that the level of deliverance for Israel was based on the fervency of his response. Because he smote the ground only three times, Israel would smite Syria only three times. Had he kept hitting the ground, deliverance would have been complete. The principle is that we are to do all we can with what we are given. Meeting the letter of the law is not sufficient for the task at hand. The parameters of victory are set by our willingness to passionately utilize all resources to advance the Kingdom of God.

In leadership, we are responsible for projecting the vision of what needs to be accomplished. We convey the task and also a general strategy. Those we are leading need to not only come up with answers, but also understand the questions of the variables involved in the mission. Helping them come to this point could be considered coaching, which is a type of leadership. Coaching involves asking questions to draw the answers out of those being coached. Coaching can be thought of as a guided process where your answers to your questions are illuminated by you through my questions. Most of that process is not about the coach, but about the one being coached (Bentley, 2019). In leadership, we are primarily facilitators to help people reach their potential.

This ties back into the fundamental differences between managers and leaders. You may have heard buzz phrases like, "managers do things right; leaders do the right thing" or "management is administration, but leadership is innovation." While there is truth to these pithy sayings, in an Apostolic context it goes much deeper than simplistic clichés. Due to the dynamic of the Spirit and objectives that transcend time and space and enter into the realm of eternity, Apostolic leadership is more profound than any other.

We might ask if leadership and management are fundamentally different, or if they require us just to focus on different things. As previously mentioned, there can be considerable overlap and both are essential for organizational success. Leaders are people of vision; managers put wheels on the vision. Numerous studies have examined the nuances among these types of leadership.

There was a study done by Harvard Business Review that looked at several leaders from various industries including business, government, Division I college sports and others. All of those interviewed described leadership as being different from management when asked in a direct question. There were varying degrees of emphasis with some simply saying, "they are different," while others answered, "absolutely." All of them clearly expressed the idea that leadership and management are distinct concepts.

These interviews also revealed nuances about performance between management and leadership. Participants described a perception of a different focus within a set of foundational elements that are common to both. For example, interviewees often mentioned the character of the leader and the positive effect that character had on followers. When describing managers, they focused more on behavior in terms of performance and achieving results. In other words, management was more closely related to achievement, an external reality. By contrast, leadership was more about an internal characteristic that manifested itself in behavior. Managers were more easily identified by what they do than by who they are. The opposite was true of leaders whose character translated into positive influence.

The study also showed that management behaviors typically center on the manager himself. These behaviors include working to gain trust, being accountable, being optimistic, being visible and providing reward and recognition. In contrast, leadership behaviors focus on the followers. This includes things like trusting people, engaging people and encouraging people. Also revealed was the fact that attitudes toward delegation and development make this distinction even clearer. Managers delegated primarily to increase efficiency while leaders delegated as a way to empower people. It is clear to see how this study is applicable to Apostolic leadership.

When we receive the Holy Ghost, we are empowered for service. There is no greater empowerment in the world. No formal or secular education, no training or mentorship can compare to the dynamic received when one is Spirit-filled. This empowerment provides the impetus whereby we are able to develop others as leaders based on the immutable principles of the Word of God.

In expanding upon the idea of behaviors that leaders use to develop people, the participants in the Harvard study identified 14 different behaviors. When talking about managers, only five behaviors emerged. In describing self-improvement, again the consensus was that managers focused more on themselves and results. For example, the focus was more on what is known as autodidactic, meaning self-taught, improvement. Examples of this include self-reflection and setting realistic expectations. Contrasted with this was the frequent approach of leaders to be more "others-focused." Leaders tend to develop themselves by learning from other people, including subordinates, by getting feedback and differing perspectives.

A primary recurring difference between managers and leaders seems to be in the emphasis of the one initiating the activity. If the focus in more on results, you are acting as a manager. If the focus is more on people, you are demonstrating leadership. Clearly, leadership in the church should be focused on the saints of God and not on self.

One thing to keep in mind as an Apostolic leader is that leadership is both about the heart and the head. Passion is vitally important, but one can possess abundant passion, yet not be particularly adept. Even worse, a passionate leader may be ignorant and not willing to learn. Having zeal is necessary, but not sufficient in itself. Zeal needs to be correctly directed in order to produce desired results.

A biblical example is found in the Apostle Paul. Even prior to his conversion, his zeal was unparalleled. He conveys this at times in his epistles describing his fervent persecution of the church. His zeal was destructive when not channeled in the right approach. The problem was that he only knew what he was taught until he gained personal revelation. This is one issue that leaders can encounter. Without proper training, some default to a trial and error approach. While this may work eventually, much unnecessary damage can occur in the interim. Further exacerbating the problem is the fact that many who are trying to be leaders have not been exposed to good leadership.

This is not necessarily their fault, as logistical concerns and other factors may have precluded consistent exposure. Thankfully, today there is a plethora of good leadership materials available in print and online.

Another potentially problematic situation for Apostolic leaders is looking to the world for leaders to emulate. This is not to say that there are no good leaders in secular environments. There are great leaders in the world who achieve tremendous success and positively impact millions of people. Some leaders head up organizations with tens of thousands of people who accomplish significant things. However, Apostolic leadership must be based entirely on biblical principles. Anything that contradicts the truths of the Bible or compromises integrity must be rejected. It is acceptable to learn from successful secular leaders, however, if their approach does not oppose godly principles. An example can be found in the Koch brothers.

Charles and David Koch own a multibillion-dollar company in Kansas. Together they are worth over $40 billion. If you study them, you will find that a lot of what they do is biblically based. As far as I know, they are not professing Christians, so their leadership style is not intentionally based on Scripture. In addition to the essential biblical aspects, what they do works because they possess a solid understanding of what motivates people. The psychological components of leadership cannot be overemphasized. Followers consistently respond when motivated appropriately. Of course, the specifics of this motivation can vary greatly due to many factors. In an Apostolic context, the over-arching motivation is the saving of souls and the perfecting of the saints. When those we lead conceptualize the magnitude of the great commission, leading them is a much easier proposition.

One could do a comprehensive study on secular leaders and gain much insight. This is a worthy endeavor which can enhance leadership ability. However, one needs to look no further than the Word of God to find exemplary leadership displayed. Rising to the top of Old Testament leadership is Moses. This remarkable leader led the children of Israel from 400 years of slavery into becoming an independent nation. In doing so he manifested multiple leadership styles necessary for dealing with varying stages of development. Myriad leadership principles could be extrapolated from his story which are applicable to leadership today.

One could study kings, priests, prophets, judges and other biblical leaders and glean much insight into both negative and positive patterns of leadership. Israel had no shortage of ungodly kings whose leadership caused the entire nation to revert to heathenistic practices. Other kings orchestrated national reform and revival because their guiding mantra was based on righteous principles. The Bible is truly a book about leadership.

Chapter Three

The Anointing

If one thing can be described as ground zero in Apostolic leadership, it is the anointing. It is from this prophetic dynamic that everything else flows. If our operation is missing this crucial element, we are reduced to the level of denominational Christianity. There is no leadership that truly exists in an Apostolic context outside of the anointing. The presence of the anointing of God is seen throughout Scripture providing leadership and empowerment.

The first instance of the anointing resting on a leader is found in Numbers chapter 11. In this context, the Lord informs Moses of His plan for effective leadership of His people. Verse 17 says, "And I will take of the spirit which is upon thee, and will put it upon them; and they shall bear the burden of the people with thee, that thou bear it not thyself alone." Verse 25 tells the fulfillment of this, "And the Lord came down in a cloud, and spake unto him, and took of the spirit that was upon him, and gave it unto the seventy elders: and it came to pass, that, when the spirit rested upon them, they prophesied, and did not cease."

We find in this instance that anointed utterance can accompany initial reception of the spirit of leadership. Another example is found in Saul's first encounter with the prophets following Samuel's declaration of the establishment of the monarchy. The prophet's explicit, detailed account of the events that would immediately transpire following the anointing for kingship included a spiritual encounter. "And the Spirit of the Lord will come upon thee, and thou shalt prophesy with them, and shalt be turned into another man" (I Samuel 10:6). When this happened, it is recorded, "And it was so that when he turned his back to go from Samuel, that God gave him another heart: and all those signs came to pass that day. And when they came hither to the hill, behold, a company of prophets met him; and the Spirit of God came upon him, and he prophesied among them" (I Samuel 10:9-10).

This transfer of prophetic anointing is seen time and again as the Lord raises up leaders in different eras of Israel's history. The spirit on Moses is imparted to Joshua prior to entering the promised land. The result is described in Deuteronomy 34:9, "And Joshua the son of Nun was full of the spirit of wisdom; for Moses had laid his hands on him." This further indicates typical results of this spiritual endowment. Wisdom, which is essential for effective leadership, was demonstrated in Joshua's encounter. It takes supernatural wisdom to effectively lead in an Apostolic environment. One may be able to learn people skills, leadership principles and many other relational qualities to enhance ability in managing a secular organization. However, when dealing with things of ultimate concern, there is no substitute for the revelation that accompanies the anointing.

The details of the account of spirit transfer between Moses and Joshua are given in the twenty-seventh chapter of Numbers. Specifically mentioned in verse 18 is the laying of Moses' hands upon Joshua to, "put some of thine honour upon him" (verse 20). The Hebrew word translated as "honour" in the King James Version is most often translated as "glory." It also appears as "majesty" in I Chronicles 29:11 referring to the splendor and authority of the Lord. The connotation is divine ruler. Navigating the tumultuous waters of spiritual enterprises necessitates supernatural empowerment.

Following the time of Joshua, Israel entered into a lengthy period in which no lasting central figurehead reigned.

Rather, the Lord raised up judges to deliver the people from oppression and to turn them back to righteousness. The length of each rule varied greatly with some reigning less than ten years and others ruling substantially longer. The specific focus for our discussion is neither their length of reign, nor their specific exploits. Rather, the common denominator lies in their source of empowerment. These were not politically elected, and neither were they appointed as progeny. Instead, the same anointing that rested upon Moses and Joshua came upon them providing the vision and empowerment for service.

This is specifically mentioned in several cases, such as with Othniel, Gideon and Jephthah. Among the most notable judges is Samson, upon whom the Spirit of God is recorded to come no less than four times in Judges 13, 14 and 15. It is only after his egregious transgression that the Spirit ceased to move on him. While the anointing of the Spirit is in operation in the lives of these judges, military exploits and national reform is the normative result. The supernatural affected the familiar.

This transfer of anointing continues during the transition of the monarchy to King David. Years prior to his ascension to the throne, David was anointed by the prophet Samuel. This anointing was particularly active in David through the manifestation of both military victories and prophetically inspired psalms. Much could be said about the variations of empowerment upon this king. Multiple roles were filled as this prophet, warrior, king, psalmist, priest would yield to the presence of God and allow divine power to flow through him for the benefit of God's people.

It might be logical to assume that the Lord would automatically transfer this anointing to the next ruler, particularly in light of David's exceptional relationship with the Lord along with his manifold accomplishments. Out of all of David's offspring, the one chosen to succeed would certainly be granted this anointing almost genetically. However, this is not the case. Solomon was anointed by Zadok the priest and Nathan the prophet, both of whom played key roles in the life of David. Yet this is the only time we find "anointing" associated with Solomon. In fact, we never find the word "spirit" and the name "Solomon" together in a single verse. We do not read of Solomon being anointed by the Spirit.

What happened at this time and in the dividing of the kingdom was that the anointing of the Spirit began to be laterally transferred from kings to prophets. This dichotomy of leadership would endure throughout the remainder of the Old

Testament as kings and priests would be used to rule God's people. When in unity, the leaders could institute spiritual and national reform and lead Israel into great times of prosperity and blessing. When in opposition, the Lord's prophets would be persecuted while backslidden kings relied on false prophets to sustain their carnal agendas.

Perhaps the clearest example of Spirit transfer is from Elijah to Elisha. So prominent is the Spirit of God on Elijah that reference is made to this anointing multiple times after his era. The canon of the Old Testament closes with the prophecy of the coming of Elijah to turn the heart of the fathers to the children and the heart of the children to the fathers (Malachi 4:5-6). This is, of course, not referring to a physical resurrection of Elijah, but rather one who would come with the same spirit as Elijah. Jesus interprets this passage in Matthew 11:13-14 in reference to John the Baptist. Indeed, John was asked specifically by the priests and Levites if he were Elijah (John 1:21). The spirit of Elijah rested as noticeably on John as it had on Elisha.

Elisha had faithfully followed Elijah during his prophetic ministry, from the time the mantle fell while Elisha was plowing with 12 yoke of oxen. His faithful service prompted the senior prophet to present a departing offer. This is found in II Kings 2:9, "And it came to pass, when they were gone over, that Elijah said unto Elisha, ask what I shall do for thee, before I be taken away from thee. And Elisha said, I pray thee, let a double portion of thy spirit be upon me." Somewhat taken aback by the request, Elijah responded with a conditional answer. "And he said, thou hast asked a hard thing: nevertheless, if thou see me when I am taken from thee, it shall be so unto thee; but if not, it shall not be so" (verse 10).

The premium Elisha placed on the anointing caused him to refuse multiple requests by Elijah for him to "tarry here" while the aged prophet completed the final tasks of his ministry. This determination was evident as well in Elisha's dismissal of the sons of the prophets' pronouncement of his master's impending departure. Nothing would dissuade the successor to abandon his opportunity for a double anointing. Ultimately, Elisha stayed the course and witnessed the catching away of his master. As a result, the mantle of anointing fully fell on Elisha. This was immediately evident by those who saw him as they emphatically observed, "The spirit of Elijah doth rest on Elisha" (I Kings 2:15). This empowerment commanded an immediate reverence as the sons of the prophets prostrated themselves before the newly anointed leader.

The leading of subsequent prophets during the reign of kings was also characterized by the anointing of the Spirit of God. Continuity of spirit empowerment can be observed in the ministries of pre-exilic, exilic and post-exilic prophets. Without regard to pedigree, vocation, position or any other irrelevant background information, the common thread that weaves the ministries together is the anointing of the Spirit.

The empowerment of the prophet Micah is explicitly described, "But truly I am full of power by the Spirit of the Lord, and of judgment, and of might" (Micah 3:8). Likewise, the prominence of the anointing is cited by Zechariah, "Not by might, nor by power, but by my Spirit, saith the Lord of hosts" (Zechariah 4:6).

Isaiah's anointing is readily identified as the actual Spirit of God in operation, such as would characterize the coming Messiah about whom he would prophesy. The Lord declares of His prophet, "Behold, my servant, whom I uphold; mine elect, in whom my soul delighteth; I have put my Spirit upon him: He shall bring forth judgment to the Gentiles" (Isaiah 42:1). Thus, Isaiah can say, "The Spirit of the Lord is upon me because the Lord hath anointed me" (Isaiah 61:1). Jesus would later ascribe this passage to Himself as he ministered in the temple (Luke 4:18-21).

Just as Jesus was the embodiment of the anointing of God, He predicted the continuance of the Spirit of God as the governing and empowering force of the New Testament church. In one of His final appearances to His disciples after His resurrection, Jesus breathed the prophetic breath in saying, "receive ye the Holy Ghost" (John 20:22). While the Spirit did not enter them at that moment, it would not be long until it was poured out in unprecedented fashion.

As Apostolics, we understand that the Holy Ghost we receive is the same Spirit of God that was initially available to all beginning on the Day of Pentecost. In His departing instructions to His followers, Jesus told them that they would receive power after that the Holy Ghost was come upon them. This power, once reserved for specific callings and certain divinely mandated individuals was now available for whosoever will. This is the same prophetic anointing that moved upon God's leaders throughout the ages.

Chapter Four

Humility

One quality that is rather elusive in secular settings, but essential in Apostolic leadership, is humility. The Bible talks extensively about lowliness, meekness and humility. There are specific commands as well as examples of humility in the annals of Scripture. There are also vivid accounts of the results of pride, which is the antithesis of humility. Pride can be thought of as an inflated view of one's self and accomplishments. In other words, pride is the idea that anything someone has done, or any valuable qualities he or she possesses, is exclusively due to personal ability. Such an inflated self-concept is fleshly and even demonic in origin.

This is fleshly as evidenced by a plethora of Scriptures. Romans 12:3 admonishes, "For I say, through the grace given unto me, to every man that is among you, not to think of himself more highly than he ought to think." The word translated as "highly" comes from a rare Greek word that only appears once in the New Testament and means, "to be overly proud, to have high thoughts." This clearly depicts someone whose ego surpasses realism. The Psalms repeatedly chronicle issues with the proud. It appears that the majority of David's dilemmas were directly related to those whose pride had overtaken them. Even a proud look is listed among the seven abominable things which the Lord hates (Proverbs 6:17).

Pride is demonic in nature as evidenced by the account of the fall of Lucifer. Isaiah vividly describes this cataclysmic event in chapter 14 of his prophecy. Verses 12-15 depict the scenario and ensuing result. Five different times this fallen angel is recorded as saying, "I will" in declaration of his futile attempt at a heavenly coup. When someone adopts an attitude of "I will ascend," or "I will exalt my throne," it is most evident what spirit they possess. Such a one will certainly meet with a bitter end if the course is not altered. Proverbs 16:18 describes the fate of the proud: "Pride goeth before destruction, and a haughty spirit before a fall." The way to promotion is not through self-exaltation, but rather through humble submission.

Arguably the most prominent example of pride in a leader's life in the Bible is that of King Saul. What is particularly tragic is the ease with which his demise can be observed. When first chosen to establish Israel's monarchy, humility was clearly present. At least three passages in I

Samuel confirm this. First, after Samuel anointed Saul to be king, Saul's recounting of the meeting did not include mention of this anointing (I Samuel 10:16). Second, when the lot fell upon the family of Matri and Saul was taken to be ruler, he was nowhere to be found (I Samuel 10:22). The prophet had to inquire of the Lord concerning his whereabouts. In an apparent act of humility, Saul had hidden himself "among the stuff." It appears that he did not feel worthy of such a noble calling and was avoiding the press involved. A third evidence of Saul's initial humility is found in Samuel's recounting of his attitude when first chosen to be king. In his rebuke for disobedience, the prophet reminded the king of a time when Saul was, "little in thine own sight" (I Samuel 15:17).

This noble characteristic was fleeting as Saul's demeanor drastically changed when an imagined threat materialized. Once David was praised more than the carnal king, pride overcame humility as jealous rage became his driving force. Ultimately, Saul was rejected as king for his disobedience concerning the annihilation of Amalek. Only then did this proud king admit his failure and sin. However, the context suggests that he was not truly repentant for his actions, but rather remorseful due to the punishment. It appears he was more concerned about the public humiliation of rejection than the egregious transgression that grieved the Lord. Tragically, this once-powerful ruler ended up seeking counsel in the house of a witch. Finally, he fell on his own sword and perished as pride won the ultimate victory.

What could have caused this anointed leader to fall from grace and go from lowly to proud? Endless speculation could ensue, but the Scripture give us some clues as to potential catalysts which could have contributed to his demise. I Samuel 13:1 says that Saul reigned two years in Israel at the point of specific actions described. In the next chapter, the Bible records that Saul built an altar unto the Lord, "the same was the first altar that he built unto the Lord" (I Samuel 14:35). This begs the question, "how can one rule over God's people for two years without building an altar?" Evidently prayerlessness and lack of sacrifice contributed to his downward spiral.

A lack of faithfulness in personal consecration greatly affects one's spirit. Had Saul been more interested in altars than in fleshly exaltation, perhaps the outcome might have been different. Had he spent more time in prayer and less in javelin throwing, he might have curbed his carnal tendencies and established a lasting lineage. Instead, the kingship shifted to a man after God's own heart whose humility is evidenced repeatedly in the accounts of his life.

The Psalms show the true spirit of David as he traverses from mountain peaks to extreme lows. From anointed personal, political and military victories, this mighty king ceased not to acknowledge the gracious hand of the Lord and to humbly worship his redeemer. Likewise, when faced with unspeakable and unjust hardships, David looked to the Lord, recognizing his inability and dependence upon God's mercy. In stark contrast to Saul, David's response when confronted by the prophet about his sin was contrite and sincere repentance. While Saul tried to justify his transgression and blame others, David confessed, "I acknowledge my transgression, and my sin is ever before me" (Psalms 51:3). He went on to admit, "against thee, thee only have I sinned, and done this evil in thy sight" (Psalms 51:4). David's desire was not to cast blame on Bathsheba for being an object of temptation. Rather, he understood the principle which James would later pen that, "every man is tempted, when he is drawn away of his own lust and enticed" (James 1:14).

Among the most remarkable displays of David's humility is found in his response to the vulnerability of Saul. Not once, but twice David was placed in a position in which he could have destroyed Saul. Supporters urged him to execute judgment, contending the Lord had delivered his enemy into his hand. In each instance, David refused to stretch forth his hand against the Lord's anointed. The humble spirit of David would not allow him to acquire the kingdom by any actions of his own. Rather, he completely trusted in the Lord for his exoneration, knowing in whom he had believed. The God who called him, anointed him and protected him was well able to perform the promise without David's assistance. This trust was rewarded, as his ascension to the throne was expedited following this most noble display of humility and dignity.

Several passages in both testaments admonish us to embrace humility. The Apostle Peter, whose impetuous nature is evidenced in the Gospels, received great revelation as the Holy Ghost taught him in his later years. He declared, "Be clothed with humility: for God resisteth the proud, and giveth grace to the humble" (I Peter 5:5). The contrast in this verse plainly states the result of both pride and humility. Which seems more appealing? Who would want the Lord's resistance when His grace is just as accessible? This conscious choice of humbling ourselves brings God's favor and grace.

Another champion of humility in the Scriptures is Moses. One would be hard-pressed to find someone with more seeming justification to be lifted up than Moses. He was chosen by the Lord for the greatest exodus in Israel's history. There was also a time when the Lord was ready to wipe out Israel for rebellion and start again with Moses (Exodus 32:10). He was described as one to whom the Lord talked face to face as a man speaks to his friend (Exodus 33:11). In Korah's rebellion, God showed His great favor on Moses and emphatically confirmed his leadership. The Bible even describes Moses as the meekest man on Earth (Numbers 12:3). His humility was unparalleled.

We are able to clearly identify the spirit of meekness through scriptural teachings and examples like David and Moses. However, most of us are not going to face an insane king determined to destroy us, or millions of murmuring people we must lead from anarchy to national identity. Inevitably, though, we will face situations that challenge our commitment to humility.

Chapter Five

Faithfulness

When we think of those who lead us spiritually, a primary characteristic that must be present is faithfulness. It is typically very unwise to place people in leadership roles who have not proven themselves. This is another biblical principle that we will examine in this chapter. Most of the time a pastor is not going to use a new convert, or sometimes even a new transfer, in a leadership role right away. The obvious reason is that these have not yet been given a chance to show faithfulness. Promoting someone too quickly is unfair to all involved. It is detrimental for the individual, as a lack of proper training and experience will often set one up for failure. Likewise, for those being led, an ill-equipped leader may be viewed as inept and call into question the wisdom of the one who promoted him or her.

Paul instructed Timothy not to promote novices to the role of bishop or pastor: "Not a novice, lest being lifted up with pride he fall into the condemnation of the devil" (I Timothy 3:6). While it may be argued that this only applies to higher-level leadership, the principle is applicable in any situation in which the likelihood of negative unintended consequences may result due to immature leadership. Granted, the potential damage inflicted is commensurate with the level of leadership. However, what should be seriously pondered is the potential ratio of positive results versus the damage which could occur. In other words, one might consider, "What is the worst thing that could happen if we let this person serve in our food pantry?" This is unlikely to have a significant impact on people's spiritualty. On the other hand, serious damage could occur if a novice were in charge of a bus route. In the work of God, collateral damage must be avoided as much as possible.

The word "novice" in I Timothy 3:6 comes from the Greek word *neophutos*. This is the word from which we get our English word "neophyte," which means someone new to a belief or skill. This is the only time this word is used in the New Testament, and it means new convert. Someone who has not yet proven faithfulness is usually not fit for much responsibility in leadership.

Perhaps you have heard of churches in which saints were allowed to sing in the choir if they showed up on Sunday night. Some pastors actually disregard their inconsistency of attendance at choir practice or even regular services. They could possibly have been missing in action for weeks, but the fact that they are there when the choir is called up somehow qualifies them for this role. This may seem too absurd to be believable, but such situations exist. This is a very blatant example of poor leadership.

As leaders, we must embrace personal faithfulness as a way of life. The epistles admonish us to practice faithfulness, "Moreover, it is required in stewards that a man be found faithful" (I Corinthians 4:2). As leaders, we are stewards of many things, not the least of which is the manifold grace of God (I Peter 4:10). We are entrusted with the highest of callings, namely helping people get to Heaven. Such an imperative necessitates a most sober commitment.

Unfortunately, in our modern society, faithfulness is not nearly as prevalent as in the past. This is evidenced by many factors including employee turnover rates, divorce rates and even a lack of commitment by some saints. It is certainly the path of least resistance to follow the wind of one's ever-changing, fickle emotions. As long as things are going well, staying is not an issue. However, when trouble comes and storms blow, the tendency for some is to seek higher ground or look for greener pastures. For the more mature, such volatile actions are recognized as a short-term fix. The reality is that trouble occurs in even the most stable of environments. The wise response is to weather the storm and keep your focus on ultimate goals. Many times the Bible says, "and it came to pass." I have never read where it says, "it came to stay."

The wise preacher lamented an unfortunate reality, "Most men will proclaim every one his own goodness: but a faithful man, who can find?" (Proverbs 20:6). This came from one who had probed all known avenues in search of truths and wisdom. His quest ended disappointedly as few were observed to possess this most noble characteristic. It is as if this elusive feature goes against human nature. As such, demonstrating faithfulness is something that must be diligently pursued in every area of life.

Of ultimate concern for Apostolic leaders is faithfulness to family. We are anointed to lead our families first. It has been astutely observed that if Noah's preaching would have saved the world, but his children would not have entered the ark, his ministry would have been a failure. In his case, this preacher of righteousness achieved the ultimate success in that those dearest to him escaped the judgment.

There are two entities hell hates more than anything: the church and the family. Jesus has already declared that the gates of hell shall not prevail against the church. However, He did not mention the family in this context. Therefore, it is incumbent upon us as Apostolic leaders to protect and defend our families as adamantly as we fight for our own souls. Jesus posed the question, "For what shall it profit a man, if he shall gain the whole world, and lose his own soul?" (Mark 8:36). A similar question could be posed: "What would it profit us if we gained the whole world, but lost our family?" Indeed the most precious commodity entrusted to us is our family.

We must be vigilant and walk circumspectly in guarding our families. This is where our leadership and influence begin. This is also where our faithfulness or lack thereof is most easily observed and emulated. This is particularly the case for those of us who have children. There is no pretense in the observation of a child. We are known even as we are to those whose innocent eyes behold the good and the evil. May we ever walk worthy of this holy vocation wherewith we are called. The Apostolic landscape has sadly been littered by those whose character was outpaced by their accomplishments. In some cases, powerful ministers have seen shipwrecked personal lives as their families were sacrificed in pursuit of other ambitions.

In pondering the enormity of the effects of faithfulness, one might wonder why the Lord would place such a premium on this attribute. Why does faithfulness mean so much to God? The answer is the same as the reason why He is so concerned about holiness. Leviticus 11:45 says, "Be ye holy, for I am holy." It is because it is God's nature. Many passages of Scripture refer to the Lord as faithful. Deuteronomy 7:9 describes the Lord as faithful. Likewise, I Corinthians 1:9 and 10:13 reiterate this truth. Hebrews 2:17 refers to Jesus as a "Merciful and Faithful High Priest." The most coveted words a child of God could ever hear from the Lord are, "Well done, thou good and faithful servant" (Matthew 25:21).

From the substantial amount of biblical teaching about faithfulness, it is evident that this should be a significant part of our character and makeup as leaders. The reality is that faithfulness is an indicator of credibility. For example, how receptive would saints be to a preacher who only showed up to church when he was preaching? For many, the first thought would be, "Where have you been?" This would likely be followed by the question, "Who are you to preach to me?" This is actually a valid consideration. If one is not found faithful in the most basic of responsibilities such as coming to the house of God, how can he or she be worthy of leadership?

Let's look a little closer at the context of the aforementioned verse in I Corinthians 4:2 which states, "Moreover, it is required in stewards that a man be found faithful." The previous verse says, "Let a man so account of us, as the ministers of Christ, and stewards of the mysteries of God." It would be easy to assume that the word "minister" refers specifically to preachers. However, the Greek word used in this passage actually means "servant" or "attendant to a king." This word is sometimes translated as "servant" in the King James Version. This understanding sheds light on the overall meaning of the passage. Likewise, the word "steward" in verse two means "a manager of household affairs." Furthermore, the word translated as faithful means "trusty, one who shows himself faithful in the transaction of business." When taken in context, the clear meaning emerges. We are to conduct the business of the King with diligence and careful attention.

While faithfulness can encompass multiple specific applications, let us look briefly at a few particularly related to spiritual disciplines. Paramount in the lives of all believers and especially in leaders is prayer. As basic as it seems, a deficiency in this crucial area can compromise leadership effectiveness, and more importantly personal consecration, more quickly than any other defect. In the absence of consistent prayer, our spirit rapidly becomes disconnected from the voice of God. How can one lead if not he or she is not able to receive vision and direction? It has been observed that if reading our Bible is like eating, then prayer is like breathing. One can endure a while without eating, but it takes very few minutes of not breathing for permanent damage to be done.

Another spiritual discipline which is obviously beneficial in our overall capacity to lead in spiritual settings is fasting. Jesus linked prayer and fasting in Mark 9:29 in reference to spiritual authority. To possess credible authority in church leadership, one must possess at least a degree of spiritual authority. Fasting heightens our sensitivity to the spirit realm. When we are able to identify the spirit behind actions and motives, wise decisions can be made in sensitive situations.

Other areas worthy of mention in a discussion about faithfulness include going to the house of God, Bible reading and multiple areas of stewardship, including time and finances. Each of these could warrant considerable exploration. However, a thorough examination is outside of the scope of our present interests.

Chapter Six

Spiritual Authority

Another key to effective Apostolic leadership is a proper understanding of spiritual authority. The Word of God repeatedly emphasizes the importance of spiritual authority and the need for obedience. There may be a temptation at times when we are about our Father's business to value our service for the Lord above our personal obedience. It is easy to justify things when we do not have an accurate perception of ourselves. This has happened for leaders who feel that their contribution to a cause makes them, in a sense, "above the law." This is a dangerous place to be.

There are scriptural accounts we can explore that underscore this principle. One well-known example is again found in King Saul. In the chapter on humility, we discussed Saul's downfall being directly related to pride. A closer look reveals the result of that pride: disobedience. There are two primary instances in which Saul's egregious rebellion resulted in tragic consequences.

The first instance is found in I Samuel chapter 13. This tells the story of a battle between Israel and the Philistines. Israel was distressed and fearful and some even hid themselves in caves. Others are recorded as following Saul "trembling" (verse 7). Hope loomed on the horizon, however, as the prophet Samuel was scheduled to arrive and offer sacrifice. Surely the presence of the man of God and the offering of the Lord would entreat divine intervention. When Samuel did not come at the appointed time, Saul took it upon himself to offer the sacrifice contrary to the Law. While it's likely that fear, confusion and doubt coalesced to render this decision feasible in his mind, the offering was nonetheless a blatant act of disobedience. To underscore this flagrant lapse of judgment, the prophet arrived immediately following the offering. His stern rebuke was a harbinger of Saul's impending fate.

The other instance in which Saul's disregard for spiritual authority is evident involves direct disobedience to the specific command of God. Reckoning day had come for the Amalekites whose judgment had long lingered since their mistreatment of God's people. The word of the Lord was explicit in commanding the annihilation of this people. Not one animal or human was to escape as the remnant was to be eradicated. There is no evidence that Saul misunderstood the mandate. Nevertheless, when Saul engaged in the battle, he felt that he had a better idea. Allegedly not for his own purposes, but rather for sacrifice, he spared the best of the flock. In an even more flagrant display of disobedience, Saul saved King Agag alive. This time Saul had crossed a line from which there was no return. In this context, Samuel declares the sacred truth that obedience is better than sacrifice (I Samuel 15:22). The critical realities of obedience to spiritual authority had never permeated the spirit of this proud king.

Other examples can be found in Scripture that speak to the importance of spiritual authority. A primary principle found in a miracle recorded in Matthew chapter eight specifically relates to authority. In this account, Jesus encountered a centurion ruler in Capernaum whose servant was in need of healing. The reaction of Jesus to the request was to go to where the servant was and heal him. The centurion recognized two vital truths in his response. First, he confesses his own unworthiness for Jesus to even enter his home. Secondly, his fundamental understanding of authority is revealed as he acknowledges that the physical presence of Jesus is not required for the miracle to take place. This soldier revealed a key principle of authority in recognizing that the word of Jesus was as powerful as the presence of Jesus. He explains his rationale in saying, "For I am a man under authority, having soldiers under me: and I say to this man, go, and he goeth; and to another, come, and he cometh; and to my servant, do this, and he doeth it" (Matthew 8:9).

The response of Jesus to this display of faith and understanding is rare in Scripture. In one of only two instances recorded, Jesus is described as marveling at the actions of someone. The other time He marveled was at unbelief. Jesus was so moved by this man's faith and understanding that he immediately performed the miracle. This revelation is worthy of a closer examination.

The centurion possessed a thorough understanding of authority because he was both under authority personally and he was in authority above other soldiers. This existence of a hierarchy was necessary for directives to be carried out. He recognized that his own authority was in many ways dependent on his personal obedience to the authorities above him. This is a critical understanding for Apostolic leaders in light of scriptural evidence.

Romans 13:1 teaches, "Let every soul be subject unto the higher powers. For there is no power but of God: the powers that be are ordained of God." In this passage we find that authority has one source. This is, of course, not to imply that everyone in authority is consciously fulfilling the will of God. We need to look no further than any government to find abuse of power in those who are pursuing their own agendas with zero regard for the will of God. What it does show us is that all authority originates from the Lord. Furthermore, anyone who is granted authority will give account for the use of that authority. This is a sobering thought indeed. Many have clamored for the bright lights and alleged prestige of leadership for self-aggrandizement. Some have found the glamour to be a bit elusive when facing the challenges of leadership. James recognized the weightiness of the leadership calling in admonishing, "Be not many masters, knowing that we shall receive the greater damnation" (James 3:1). To whom much is given, much is required.

Paul expounded on this truth in continuing, "Whosoever therefore resisteth the power, resisteth the ordinance of God: and they that resist shall receive to themselves damnation" (Romans 13:2). Now we see the gravity of disobedience come into focus. Abuse of authority is a serious offense. As leaders, with or without a title or position, we inherently possess some degree of authority. This authority usually translates to influence. When we rebel against the authority over us, there is often a compounded effect. It is difficult to expect compliance from subordinates when we ourselves are not obedient to authority.

As evidenced in the actions of Saul, regardless of motives, rebellion against authority is tantamount to rebellion against God's authority. David recognized this in his sin with Bathsheba. In his repentant psalm, he confessed, "against thee, thee only have I sinned" (Psalm 51:4). At first glance this does not seem accurate. There were many people against whom David sinned including Bathsheba, Uriah, even Joab. Despite this reality, the crux of the matter was that the Lord was the one against whom he sinned. Recognizing this ultimate violation of authority, David was able to rightly summarize his error.

Understanding authority is critical for anyone who desires to be used of God. At the most basic level, every saint, regardless of aspirations, must learn obedience to spiritual authority. Failure to do so jeopardizes salvation. All things are created by God's authority and all physical laws of the universe are maintained by His authority. This is what is meant when Hebrews says, "Upholding all things by the word of His power" (1:3). Paul reiterates this truth in declaring, "For by Him were all things created, that are in heaven, and that are in earth, visible and invisible, whether they be thrones, or dominions, or principalities, or powers: all things were created by Him and for Him" (Colossians 1:16-17). This verse speaks explicitly about authority.

Specifically identified in this passage are thrones, dominions, principalities and powers. Powers in this verse comes from *exousia* in the Greek. Most of the time when we see the word authority in the New Testament, it is *exousia*. The word power is most often from the Greek word *dunamis*. For example, both words are used in Luke 9:31 when Jesus called His disciples together and gave them power and authority over all devils, and to cure disease. In this instance, power was *dunamis* and authority was *exousia*. These words refer to both the ability and the right to exercise power.

A modern example might be if you owned a 600 horsepower 7 series BMW. You have the power to go 150 miles per hour, but you do not have the authority to do so. If you decide to try it, you will probably soon see some flashing lights behind you. So we find there is a difference between power and authority. Just because one has the ability to act, does not necessarily equate to the right to act. This authority is not gained merely by credentials or titles, but rather this authority comes from the Lord.

The Apostle Paul understood this aspect of authority. In the account of his conversion in Acts chapter nine we find that Ananias was the one whom the Lord used to initially make contact with Saul, who would become known as Paul. Ananias is mentioned only one time outside of this conversion account, and that is when Paul is retelling the story in chapter 22. He is by no means a main character in Scripture. There is no indication that he is a pastor or leader. Acts 22:12 says that he was a devout man who had a good report among the Jews. By all indications he was an average saint who had a strong relationship with the Lord. Yet Paul recognized his authority after Jesus spoke to him on the road to Damascus and instructed him to go to the house of Ananias. Paul did not argue with Ananias or demand to see his credentials. Paul did not try to pull rank by declaring he was taught by Gamaliel himself. Rather, he humbly submitted to the words of this saint and experienced salvation.

The principle seen in the story of this encounter between Ananias and Saul is that when the Word of God comes to us, we are not merely obeying a man, but rather God's authority in that man. Perhaps you have heard some declare that the preaching of their pastor was just the opinion of a man. This is a grave mistake. The Thessalonians were commended when Paul said, "For this cause also thank we God without ceasing, because, when ye received the Word of God which ye heard of us, ye received it not as the word of men, but as it is in truth, the Word of God, which effectually worketh also in you that believe" (I Thessalonians 2:13). This clearly teaches that the Word preached did not originate with man's authority, but with God's. Your pastor is representative of God's authority in your life, and you must learn to obey.

Obedience to the voice of God is clearly the most vital theme throughout Scripture. If Noah had not built the ark exactly to the specifications directed by the Lord, it would not have weathered the storm. Likewise, when we do not obey the voice of God in our lives, we subject ourselves to many unnecessary storms. In Acts 27:21, Paul reminds the distraught sailors facing a raging storm, "Sirs, ye should have hearkened unto me." He was reiterating the fact that he had previously warned them that he perceived the voyage would be, "with hurt and much damage" (Acts 27:10). Never underestimate the perception of the man of God. "Nevertheless," the narrative continues, "the centurion believed the master and the owner of the ship, more than those things which were spoken by Paul" (Acts 27:11). Shipwreck could have been avoided with a simple act of obedience.

Obedience to spiritual authority is so critical that everyone must learn it. Even Jesus learned obedience, according to Hebrews 5:8, by the things which He suffered. In the Garden of Gethsemane, the man Christ Jesus submitted His will to the will of the Spirit. How can we assume that such obedience would not be required of us if God in the flesh offered this perfect example?

Matthew chapters 26 and 27 record the twofold judgment which Jesus faced after His arrest. Before the high priest there was religious judgment. Before Pilate there was political judgment. Jesus did not answer Pilate in regards to the political examination. In all three of the synoptic accounts, when asked if He was king of the Jews, Jesus is recorded as answering merely, "Thou sayest." When told by Pilate that he had the authority to let him go or crucify Him, Jesus' response was, "Thou couldest have no power at all against me, except it were given thee from above" (John 19:11). Jesus was referring back to the original source of power, which is God.

Paul also faced judgment before the high priest in Acts chapter 23. The Scripture records that Paul spoke against the high priest before he realized who he was. After this revelation, he even quoted Scripture defending the fact that he would not have reviled him had he been aware of his office. The idea is that religious authority was highly respected by both Jesus and Paul. Civil authority is also to be respected and obeyed. However, the laws of God always supersede the laws of man. This is what is meant in Acts 5:29, when Peter says that he ought to obey God rather than man.

In most instances, the laws of man are not going to violate the laws of God. Therefore, obedience to these laws is tantamount to obeying the ultimate authority of the Lord. As Apostolic leaders our submission to authority is necessary not only for our own sakes, but also for the sake of those we lead. Understanding the power of influence exerted through our example should be a pertinent enough reason to practice genuine obedience and submission.

Though it may seem semantical, there is actually a significant difference between obedience and submission. Obedience is an act; submission is a spirit. One can comply with rules with a contumacious spirit. However, when we are genuinely submissive, we will not just perform the duty required, but we will do so without a bad attitude and without looking for a way around the duty. On a side note, this is why ruling with an iron fist is ineffective. People who are unwillingly subjugated look for any opportunity to disobey and rebel. Leading by love and sincere concern is the preferred method of achieving results beyond obligatory obedience.

Chapter Seven

Motivation

The idea of motivation is key in leadership. Simply put, people will rarely do things without some type of motivating force. There are certainly times that saints of God do things out of obligation without a personal desire or ambition. However, this type of behavior may technically accomplish the job at hand but will not produce lasting results or residual willingness. To see people excited about doing kingdom work requires ongoing motivation. While sometimes external motivators can be effective, it is not a dog and pony show that creates sustainable motivation. Rather, lasting motivation happens when followers are inspired and possess a burden for the work of God.

One primary way to create a burden is through exposure. I have seen carnal young people take a mission's trip in which they are exposed to deplorable conditions of humanity. This can happen in another country or even in major cities in the United States. Seeing the fallen state of our fellow man in his seemingly inescapable plight causes an awakening of the need for the Gospel. This often translates to a burden to work in the kingdom at the local assembly. This kind of internal motivation can prove to be a powerful impetus which results in soul-winning efforts. Someone who was previously not interested in bus ministry, for example, might return from a trip to New York with an insatiable desire to help hurting and confused young people who are looking to the world for answers. Learning to capitalize on this motivation is the job of the leader.

Another powerful motivator is the preaching of the Word of God. How many messages have been preached about the coming of the Lord, impending judgment, lost humanity, or other such convicting realities that have stirred our hearts to action? It has often been said that we get what we preach. Is it any wonder that churches that never preach about soul-winning or evangelism rarely see breakthroughs or revival? We could probably all point to sermons we have heard that impacted us greatly to the point of action. I can remember a message by Wayne Huntley in the mid 1990's that he preached at a camp meeting in Michigan. It was so inspiring that I prepared a survey intended for witnessing and distributed it the following work day. What happened was that I was motivated by the revelation of responsibility to reach people with the Gospel. The burden was so strong that it overcame personal pride as well as suspicion from those who questioned my motives. The understanding that I was a steward of the one plan of salvation was sobering and awe-inspiring.

Admittedly, few people live in the realm of this level of motivation every day. As such, it is incumbent upon leaders to provide ongoing motivation for spreading the Gospel. Anyone who has been filled with the Holy Ghost possesses the ability to be a witness, as Acts 1:8 declares that we shall receive power after that the Holy Ghost has come upon us. A sincere child of God does not need a seminar on soul-winning and evangelism to be equipped to witness. All that is needed is motivation and direction. Motivation without direction is frustration. Therefore, a leader's role is twofold in needing to not only inspire followers to action, but also to show appropriate means whereby the mission can be accomplished.

The area of motivation is one in which Apostolic leadership differs greatly from secular leadership. In the corporate world, many studies have been conducted in an effort to find the silver bullet of motivation. Results vary greatly within industries as well as across various disciplines. The natural assumption in a corporate setting would be that money would likely consistently top the list. Surprisingly, although this often ranks near the top of motivators, other less tangible stimuli often rank above income. Things like time off and flexibility of schedule repeatedly appear as primary motivating factors for professionals. The reality is that having the freedom to live our lives, spend time with our families and do things we enjoy provide much more lasting satisfaction than just padding our bank account. Businesses that want to attract and retain quality employees pay attention to this reality and attempt to structure their employment benefit packages accordingly.

What does this look like in the Kingdom of God? In most cases, few individuals besides the pastor are paid to do the work of God. Of course, there are sometimes assistants, music staff, or other paid positions, but in a typical Apostolic church, saints are not compensated for service like those in business are. So if we, as leaders, do not have an external reward system for motivation, how difficult is it to mobilize the collective resources of the church for kingdom expansion? Besides the motivators previously mentioned, there are intangible motivators we can offer to promote allegiance and desire for continued service.

As previously stated, leaders go to the level of inspiration. To do so, we must connect with people at a spiritually cellular level. While this may sound confusing if not incredulous, the reality is that human nature craves acceptance and validation. Insincere leaders have long abused this reality by manipulating followers for personal gain. Sadly, charlatans have existed in both the church and the world for a long time. There have been churches that have suffered spiritual abuse rendering them essentially incapable of trusting leaders. Some Apostolic churches have had five or more pastors within a 10-year period. While many of these have not intentionally harmed the church or its members, the reality is that scenarios like this can create a culture of cynicism that can be difficult to overcome. A pastor or leader in such a situation needs to first build trust through sincere and genuine interaction. Patience is key as we acknowledge that processing the hurts takes time.

Thankfully, most Apostolic churches do not face the type of corporate dysfunction described above. Still, the need for trust is present, as attempting to do business in deep waters of the Spirit requires a unity not typically found without much intentional cultivation. As leaders in the church, our everyday actions can affect the motivation of those under our care. When pastors and other leaders in the church seem aloof and disconnected, motivation suffers. The appearance of living in an ivory tower as an untouchable resonates negatively with most saints. Followers want to see their leadership in the trenches fighting the good fight alongside them. This causes them to feel as if the mission is not resting squarely on their shoulders, but rather that they are partnering with God's anointed leader and significantly contributing to the great cause of kingdom work.

Besides being visible, touchable and personal, leaders can motivate those they serve in other ways as well. One way is in simply acknowledging the value of the work being done. This does not have to be a grandiose announcement to the church extolling the virtues of an individual recognizing the results of a ministry. It can be something as simple as verbally expressing appreciation and asking about the welfare of the ministry being performed. If time and schedules permit, a leader could meet with one who is focusing efforts in a specific area and discuss what is working and what could be improved. This might take place over coffee or lunch in an hour or less. For a minimal investment of a leader's time much can be accomplished. First, this negates the likelihood of someone yielding to the temptation to think of himself as an island. When a leader takes time to engage in a discussion of a follower's work, this shows concern and backing for the work being done. It is easy to get discouraged and feel like what we are doing is unimportant or overlooked. Also, such an encounter validates the worth of the individual in more than a corporate way. While it is beneficial to commend a department or congregation as a whole, the effort it takes to individually connect goes to a more personally motivating level.

Investing time in individuals can create a type of bond that is inherently motivating. When someone feels that he or she is needed, personal responsibility results in inspiring motivation and camaraderie. This can also be contagious as the one being motivated is likely to help others catch the vision. This can create a ripple effect in which other saints desire to get on board and plug into ministry opportunities.

Time invested in the lives of followers does not have to be excessive to be effective. A simple phone call to see how someone is faring can demonstrate genuine concern which can be impacting. Likewise, something as old-fashioned as sending a card with a personal note can help people stay motivated by making them feel appreciated. Such deliberate, personal actions help create a culture of allegiance that translates to sustained motivation.

Also, many pastors have seen success in having annual retreats or periodic appreciation dinners. Spending time with fellow laborers to celebrate successes and plan new strategies can pay residual dividends. Unity is a key in the work of God. Strategically utilizing resources to motivate followers to consistent action is a worthwhile endeavor.

The topic of motivation warrants a closer look at specific examples of leaders' attempts to inspire those under their care. Stories can be found in secular settings as well as in the Word of God. As kingdom business is rightfully described as a warfare, it is appropriate to look at illustrations of a military nature.

In America's most tumultuous time in its young history, the nation was divided over seemingly irreconcilable issues that would change the course of its destiny. In its bloodiest conflict ever that would take more American lives than any other, the North and South engaged in the Civil War. By divine appointment, Abraham Lincoln was at the helm guiding the Union forces in preserving the fledgling union. As brother fought against brother, motivation suffered as victory seemed elusive for both sides. In the midst of disheartening circumstances, President Lincoln would often visit the troops to see how they were faring. He understood that the fate of the nation was going to be determined by their actions.

It is well-documented that President Lincoln would spend hours at the War Department's telegraph room to ensure immediate access to the most current news from the battlefield. He would also meet with key leaders such as cabinet members and generals in various places to provide real-time leadership. The president would also personally visit battlefields to observe firsthand the condition of the troops and assess strategies.

One Lincoln biographer recounts a story of the President removing a general from office due to egregious mistakes that were demoralizing for the troops (Phillips, 1992). General John C. Fremont, who was leading the Department of the West, was being replaced by General David Hunter. In a letter to Hunter, Lincoln wrote, "He [General Fremont] is losing the confidence of men near him, whose support any man in his position must have to be successful. His cardinal mistake is that he isolates himself and allows nobody to see him; and by which he does not know what is going on in the very matter he is dealing with."

The principle for Apostolic leaders is that in order to know what is transpiring in the efforts of those we lead, we must presence ourselves in their situations. When possible, a leader should be involved in the actual ministry as it is taking place. For example, a Sunday School superintendent should periodically visit the classrooms of the teachers. This gives him valuable exposure to the inner workings of the ministry. It also allows a visible connection with the teachers and students. Such exposure is invaluable in gaining an understanding of the needs of that particular ministry.

A biblical example of a leader staying with the troops can be found in the rebuilding of the walls of Jerusalem as recorded in the book of Nehemiah. The efforts of the Jews to repopulate their homeland after Babylonian exile were being resisted by enemy forces. The antagonists used psychological warfare such as insults, threats and intimidation in an effort to thwart the progress of God's people. Rather than hide in the comfort of Shushan the palace, Nehemiah worked alongside those he was leading providing onsite leadership. His presence no doubt provided security, stability and motivation for the troops. In addition, his being there allowed the workers immediate access to direction. When Sanballat and Tobiah hurled their insults, the seasoned leader was available to respond with holy boldness and declaration of his God-inspired mission. This response strengthened and encouraged the workers who otherwise might have been intimidated into abandoning the project.

Of particular note in chapter four is the spiritual response of the leader when faced with opposition. Nehemiah appealed to the Lord for direction in praying, "Hear, O our God; for we are despised: and turn their reproach upon their own head, and give them for a prey in the land of captivity" (Nehemiah 4:4). Verse six shows the results of the leader's prayer, "So we built the wall: and all the wall was joined together unto the half thereof: for the people had a mind to work." This begs the question, "Would the people have had a mind to work if not for the strength gained by the presence of the leader?"

As with any aspect of spiritual warfare, there will be opposition to motivation. Realities such as burnout, fatigue, discouragement and other malevolent emotions are often encountered by leaders. It is possible to give ourselves completely to a ministry only to face discouragement when results do not come as quickly as desired. In life it seems that most things take longer than expected. Unforeseen obstacles and setbacks often surface in any project. The work of the Lord is no exception. In actuality, this circumstance is often exacerbated as the added element of spiritual opposition coincides with natural resistance.

Examples can be found in initiatives of varying degrees. An obvious example might be a pastor engaged in a building program. Few pastors ever report a flawless process when constructing a new edifice for worship. Rather, many pastors testify of the devils they fought, along with the internal and external struggles the church endured during that season. Costs often exceed initial estimates, contractors run behind and materials get stolen all while saints have marriage issues, children rebel and the music department suffers disunity. The challenge to stay focused and motivated surfaces daily. While this may be an extreme example, pastors are not the only ones who face resistance and the possibility of burnout due to ambitious projects. Other leaders in the church also encounter opposition to the work of God.

Ministries ranging from Sunday School to outreach, from youth to media face the threat of fatigue and the temptation to quit. The precious saints involved in these and other ministries need to stay motivated in order to continue involvement that is personally fulfilling and meaningful. Incumbent upon the leader is the task of keeping others engaged and motivated.

One circumstance that often leads to burnout is overworking in a ministry. For example, someone may start out with much zeal for a bus route and declare that he or she is going to do this route every week indefinitely. If the children on the route become unmanageable and the driver begins to resent the obligation, the likelihood of quitting altogether becomes much greater. A simple solution is to mandate breaks periodically, such as monthly, so that the driver can enjoy Sunday morning service without being encumbered with the extra responsibility of having to arrive early and possibly miss the altar call to ensure students are returned home on time.

Other examples might include too many services assigned to security, media or ushering. If someone is always expected to be in the sound booth, he or she does not have the freedom to go to the altar after the message or engage fully in the worship portion of the service. Likewise, if someone's desire to work in protecting the church keeps him or her from participating in the service unencumbered, becoming lukewarm spiritually might result. The job then becomes an obligation and potentially a mask for one's weakening spiritual condition. A rotating schedule can prevent this and keep those passionate about certain ministries motivated and excited.

Chapter Eight

Responding to Conflict

In any leadership role, including in an Apostolic context, conflict will arise. Much conflict is healthy and can lead to growth, revelation and maturity. In many cases, however, conflict is the result of carnal people with personal agendas. Attacks that come against us often test our spirit. As leaders our knee-jerk reaction might be, "who do they think they are?" when someone comes against us. It has been observed that a true test of being a servant is how you react when you are treated like one. No one appreciates disrespect and the temptation is to respond in kind. Nevertheless, as Apostolic leaders we must be mindful of our reaction to conflict, understanding both the interplay of spiritual forces and the potential for irreparable damage. Remember, we are dealing with matters of ultimate concern and must conduct ourselves appropriately.

There are antagonistic forces both naturally and spiritually in the work of God. Not everyone wants us to succeed. While opposition from people comes and goes, the spiritual forces of darkness are incessantly at work to sabotage our efforts. There is no biblical reference to the Kingdom of God being easily obtained with minimal resistance. There is, however, a direct powerful quote from the Lord of lords pertaining to spiritual advancement. Jesus said, "The kingdom of heaven suffereth violence, and the violent take it by force" (Matthew 11:12). The reality is greatly intensified in the arena of leadership. The work of God is described by the Apostle Paul repeatedly as warfare (II Corinthians 10:4, I Timothy 1:18, II Timothy 2:3-4). War involves conflict.

In years past, attempts to stop the church were blatant and often physical. Persecution the early church faced included horrific acts of physical torture. Likewise, in the more recent past, persecution was similar, though obviously not as violent as Pentecostalism's mainstream resurgence shook America in the early part of the 20th century. Today, our adversary is often much more subtle in opposition. Conflict usually goes much deeper than physical altercations and involves manipulation and insidious clandestine tactics.

There are steps that can be followed when considering a response to personal conflict. A good starting point when faced with a personal attack or accusation is to attempt to honestly assess if there could be any truth to the accusation. Admittedly, this is easier said than done, as none of us can see ourselves objectively. If we are able to evaluate the claim, perhaps there is some semblance of validity even if shrouded in vitriol and inaccurate perceptions. It has been well established that perception in many cases is reality. Even if someone is completely off in their perception, to them it is reality. Changing this perception can be a daunting task, particularly if the accuser is not willing to honestly consider a conflicting view.

To even give consideration to the merit of a personal attack takes a measure of humility. This is a good time to take personal inventory. Not only as leaders, but as humans, we have blind spots. There are most likely areas in our lives that we cannot see clearly. Sometimes those closest to us may try to alert us to these weaknesses, but often the tendency is to dismiss such claims as nagging or nitpicking. Yet if we can bring ourselves to at least view the evidence, we might be surprised. Again, this is not an easy task as ego and pride can collaborate to sabotage the effort. When an attack comes, it is often wise to give it some thought. The best way to do this is in prayer. God knows our thoughts though they be afar off. In our sincere quest for truth, the Lord has a way of gently revealing things of which we may not be aware.

The specific conflict being addressed in this juncture is that of accusation or outside attack. One example of conflict might be someone criticizing how we run our department in the church. Another could be the accusation that we are trying to promote ourselves or jockey politically for self-aggrandizement. Many other potential scenarios could be suggested. The issue is not so much the specifics of the attack, but rather the proper response to such.

In cases like these, one positive is that we have time to formulate a response. There is usually no need to rush unless others are going to be quickly affected. Therefore, it is critical that we be calculated in our response. Even before that, it might be good to determine if a response is warranted at all. In some instances, the attack may be nothing more than a disgruntled individual whose common practice is to criticize and whose credibility has been diminished to the point that a response would only dignify the injustice of the accusation. There are times in which a response might only worsen the situation. Some things have a tendency to work themselves out if left untouched. Of course, determining this course of action takes wisdom and discernment.

James 1:19 teaches, "Let every man be swift to hear, slow to speak, slow to wrath." This admonishes us not to be hasty in our response. The apostle continued in saying, "For the wrath of man worketh not the righteousness of God" (verse 20). Clearly a response in anger is not likely to fulfill God's purpose in the situation. Rather, being slow to speak and slow to wrath is a much more viable option for peaceful resolution.

It is also sometimes wise to give the benefit of the doubt when possible. There are times when the information we have received may not be entirely accurate. It is easy for things to be taken out of context. Furthermore, we do well to assume that the one causing the conflict is not our enemy. This may not be the case, but initially acknowledging this possibility can curb our natural tendency toward retaliation. They might just be hurt or angry about something they perceive you have done. Hurting people are often fearful people, who lash out as a result. Unresolved anger can lead to unintended consequences. Judgment can be skewed and they start throwing javelins.

Another helpful tactic in formulating a response is to consider the source. This may seem harsh on the surface, as if advocating the proposition that opinions of some do not matter. What is meant by that statement is that there are people whose judgment and perception have been warped, rendering them incapable of sound assessment. As previously stated, some attack out of fear or hurt. Others make ill-informed judgments based on limited information. Many other possible factors could exist that can cause an otherwise well-meaning saint to act irrationally.

Another facet of considering the source is to determine how much influence the accuser has. How many people could be unknowingly swept into this conflict, simply because the perpetrator is charismatic and can easily convince others of the idea? This is a valid concern as countless examples could be cited of essentially innocent bystanders being caught in the crossfire. The likelihood of others being affected certainly impacts the swiftness of our response.

Conflict that isn't handled properly can damage pride and reputations. Worse yet, this could cause someone to backslide. You may be proven wrong in your generous act of giving the benefit of the doubt. However, it most cases, this is a wise first step while we gather more information and take time to pray about it. It is never wise to shoot first and ask questions later. Just the simple actions of following the preceding steps in conflict resolution could give the accuser time to realize the error of his or her ways and repent. Swift and uncalculated judgment can eliminate this possibility and deliver a fatal blow.

Of course, one obvious move to make when considering how to resolve a conflict is to seek godly counsel. If you are a pastor, there are elders in your life to whom you are accountable and from whom you seek direction at times. If you are a local leader under a pastor, it is necessary to speak with your pastor for counsel. Many times the pastor has much more information than we might have. This knowledge can shed valuable light on the overall condition of the person causing conflict. Access to a greater understanding of the bigger picture can be invaluable in determining if and how to respond.

Another good practice in resolving conflict is to avoid involving other people unnecessarily. Our natural tendency is to draw battle lines and try to get others to join our side. This is unwise in many ways. Informing others of the conflict without just cause draws people in who likely have no reason or ability to contribute to resolution. Inevitably, these end up choosing sides. They may even do this subconsciously because it is human nature to form judgments based on the information we have. A third party may have had a negative encounter previously with the accuser and have an interest in vengeance. Involving someone like this will only cause disunity.

Preserving unity is a primary interest in Apostolic leadership. Churches do not grow and ministries do not flourish in atmospheres of incessant discord. Jesus said, "Blessed are the peacemakers: for they shall be called the children of God" (Matthew 5:9). Notice he did not say, "peacekeepers." The United Nations has a division known as the peacekeepers. Their governing principles include consent of the parties, impartiality and non-use of force (United Nations, 2019). The focus of this entourage is based on the assumption that peace already exists. When facing conflict as Apostolic leaders, the need is for peacemaking. Romans 12:18 teaches, "If it be possible, as much as lieth in you, live peaceably with all men."

Another thing to remember is to keep the scenario in perspective. What does it really mean in the grand scheme of things? Does it have the potential to split the church, or just bruise your ego? This suggestion is not to belittle any conflict, but rather to encourage one to weigh it against the big picture. A key understanding in leadership is knowing what to overlook. Sometimes picking our battles is the best course of action.

Finally, after examining the conflict in light of the preceding suggestions, it is often necessary to take action. It is often in our best interest to confront the accuser as objectively as possible. Rather than coming in with "guns blazing," as leaders we should engage in a level-headed and calm manner. This is obviously easier said than done as emotions will, no doubt, enter the equation. Things to consider are what our spirit and motives are like. Am I really wanting reconciliation, or just to prove I am right? Am I trying to protect my kingdom, or advance the Kingdom of God? What matters most? Winning and being right? Or does the welfare of the souls involved merit the highest concern?

Chapter Nine

Goal Setting and Assessment

One intangible, yet inescapable responsibility of leaders in Apostolic churches is the need to cast vision. Those we lead need to see a picture of the God-inspired goal. Obtaining this vision and direction comes through spiritual formation and seeking the Lord. Once the vision is obtained, it must then be articulated to those who will carry out the mandate. Whatever the vision, leaders must formulate a plan for the goal's implementation. This includes both short-term and long-term goals as well as a means of assessing those goals. This necessitates parameters within which objectives must be framed.

An acronym has been developed that summarizes a framework for goals: SMART (Brock and Hundley, 2016). Each letter represents an aspect of the goal that must be present. There are variations of this acronym, but the general idea stays the same. In one variation, the S stands for "specific," the M for "measurable," the A for "attainable," the

R for "relevant," and the T for "timely." The concept is sound and, in many ways, applicable to Apostolic ministry.

It is not difficult to define a specific goal. This simply entails spelling out what is to be accomplished. For example, a youth pastor might have a goal to double the youth group within a year. If the current youth group consisted of 25 members, to double it would mean that an additional 25 would need to be added. Likewise, if a Sunday School superintendent wanted to go from five bus routes to ten within a certain timeframe, the specific goal would be to add five new bus routes. Any number of scenarios could be presented with simple calculations to frame the specifics of the goal. In contrast, a leader might proclaim a general desire to see the youth group grow or to add bus routes to the current Sunday school ministry. While this might be thought of as a goal, in reality it's just zealous ambition without a specific target. Such an ambition, while admirable and necessary, is difficult to assess. Furthermore, goals that are not specific are not as easy to celebrate. If one year after casting this general vision, one person was added to the youth group, will there be rejoicing over meeting such a goal? Specificity provides a target at which to shoot.

Aspects of determining a specific goal include assessment of resources involved as well as timeframes. Essentially this amounts to determining what the goal looks like. What exactly is to be accomplished, who will be involved, how long it will take to accomplish and other questions along these lines help frame the specificity of the desired result. It is also during this initial phase when one determines if adequate resources are available. Setting a goal too high can almost guarantee failure from the beginning. This is not to negate the faith element, which will be discussed later. Rather, realistic assessment is a wise and biblical approach showing discretion. Jesus asked the question, "For which of you, intending to build a tower, sitteth not down first, and counteth the cost, whether he have sufficient to finish it?" (Luke 14:28).

The next important ingredient in setting a goal is to ensure that it is measurable. This dovetails with the idea of the goal being specific. If an objective is not quantifiable, it is difficult to ascertain when it is achieved. This does not mean that goals can never contain any subjective element. What it means is that there needs to be some way to determine the goal has been met. The most obvious example would be a numerical goal such as those described earlier. It can also be time related, such as completing phase one of a building project.

One benefit of having measurable goals is that visible progress helps keep those involved motivated. If a building program, for example, sees no observable progress for a long period of time, people can become disheartened. This discouragement can easily translate to complaining, second-guessing or even withholding funds. When a project is being completed incrementally and small successes can be celebrated, saints remain focused and determined to stay the course.

The third component of goal setting is to make sure the goal is attainable. This may be a bit more difficult to define than some of the others, since making this determination is somewhat subjective. An attainable goal is one which can be reached without depending too heavily on miraculous intervention. This is certainly a fine line and is worthy of a bit of qualification. What is not meant by an attainable goal is one that can necessarily be accomplished with only current available resources. For example, if a church waits until it has a million dollars in the bank before embarking on a building program, no goal is needed. It's simply a matter of lining up the contractors and writing the checks. This requires neither faith nor hope, but is based on what is seen. Paul told the Romans that, "Hope that is seen is not hope: for what a man seeth, why doth he yet hope for?" (Romans 8:24). What is meant by an attainable goal is one that requires vision, faith and cooperation from followers.

The faith element is certainly a primary difference between goal setting in the corporate world and that in an Apostolic church. We understand that with God all things are possible. The Word also tells us that if we agree together in touching anything, it shall be done (Matthew 18:19). The idea of determining attainable goals is not to negate faith. The Lord desires for us to believe Him for big things. James said we have not because we ask not (James 4:2). Notwithstanding the necessary role of faith in all kingdom work, this needs to be tempered with discretion and prayerful planning. We know God can do anything, but does this mean we should quit our jobs and pray for groceries to be delivered to our doorstep daily by angels? That is admittedly an extreme example, however the concept applies in goal setting. Many of us have seen the Lord do the miraculous when the church note was due or the enormity of the need appeared to swallow us up. Provision is

God's specialty and these interventions increase faith and propel His mission forward. Nevertheless, to begin an initiative in an ill-advised manner can often result in the opposite effect. Pentecost does not need a Stone's Folly to distract us in harvesting in the end time.

The fourth letter of the SMART acronym stands for relevant. This one is of particular importance in Apostolic ministry. As stated previously, the two primary objectives of the church are to reach the lost and perfect the saints. Therefore, every goal set should contribute to this overall mission. As with the idea of passion-based ministries discussed in a previous chapter, initiatives of Apostolic ministry must coincide with the vision of the church. This can exist in varying degrees as some goals may not immediately appear to contribute significantly in moving the church forward. An example might be a goal of organizing teams for a monthly fellowship dinner. To some this might appear to be just another obligation of time, when in reality it is promoting unity among the body.

It is entirely possible for a church today to be swept away by the latest trends and fashions of mainline denominational Christianity. There are no shortage of non-

Apostolic churches that embark on crusades to emulate the world and its entertainment to attract a crowd. Props and paraphernalia formerly relegated to venues such as sports stadiums and rock concerts have become more prevalent in some churches. This begs the question, "Are these new additions relevant to what we are trying to accomplish?" The answer would vary based on what the objective is. If the primary desire of a congregation is to see inflated numbers and increased giving, then perhaps these ancillary tokens are of value. However, if a church—especially an Apostolic church—stays true to its mission, setting a goal of raising $50,000 for flashing lights is not relevant to the cause.

An additional consideration of the relevance of a goal is the appropriateness of the season. Some goals may meet all of the other criteria, but may not be the best course of action at the moment. Churches go through seasons. There are seasons of sowing, seasons of trials, seasons of proclamation, seasons of possession, seasons of reaping and so on. When a goal is set by a leader, be it the pastor, department head or another, there needs to be prayerful consideration of the season the church is in. If, for example, a fledgling church has struggled for its first three years with inconsistent attendance and finances, it is likely not the season to cast a vision to build a new sanctuary.

The final letter of the goal setting acronym stands for timely. In a broad sense, this means that a definable goal should have a type of end date. There are admittedly many variables in any scenario so to set a hard, fast date for achievement is often not wise, if even possible. This principle is applicable in most cases, however, since realistic timelines can usually be determined. Previous examples focused on numerical growth or building programs. Another example could be a goal of ten outreach efforts in a year. The director of the program could evenly distribute dates throughout the year and promote them in the weeks leading up to the event. Built into the schedule could be the exclusion of busy times such as the peak of summer or the holidays.

Goals such as the one described above project a realistic timeframe in which the activity can be completed. This is beneficial for several reasons. For one, it keeps the initiative in front of the people. Secondly, it gives multiple opportunities for people to get involved. If there were only two or three scheduled times for outreach, odds are that there would be several people for whom the dates would present a conflict.

Furthermore, this approach theoretically involves a greater number of people as different dates typically translate to a more diverse group of attendees.

Setting goals using the framework of the SMART method can help Apostolic ministries be organized and efficient in their efforts. Random and uncalculated use of resources is poor stewardship. We need to invest what the Lord has entrusted us with so that we can maximize the return on the investment. When Apostolic ministries prayerfully and wisely utilize available resources, the Lord blesses our efforts. This conversation also necessitates a word about assessment.

From time to time leaders have to assess the progress of goals. Having a game plan formulated beforehand aids in this process immensely. There is a temptation when assessing progress to be idealistic. Everyone wants their efforts to succeed. When things are behind schedule or not producing desired results, there may be a propensity to make excuses or even falsely represent progress. This is easier is some situations than in others. Goals that are not as prominent in the public eye can be minimized so that insufficient progress can be shielded. Other, more visible initiatives such as a building program are more difficult to spin. The best practice is to be honest in our assessment of where we are in terms of achieving a goal.

Honesty in assessment is necessary and proper for many reasons. First, a lack of transparency about the utilization of resources in a church can breed distrust. Few things will stop revival faster than disgruntled saints who are suspicious about what is going on. As stewards chosen by the Lord to engage in His business, we owe it to all involved to be upfront and to operate with integrity. Also, denying the obvious issues that are truncating our progress only exacerbates the negative effects. If something isn't working, the best course of action is to analyze why it isn't working. Trying to sweep problems under the rug instead of facing them head-on only delays the inevitable result of failure.

Sometimes the reason why an initiative is struggling is easily identified. Maybe a small miscalculation was made in planning that is easily corrected. Perhaps wrong personnel are involved who are inept at teamwork and are creating unnecessary hindrances for others involved. In some cases, the execution of the task may be inherently flawed. In other cases, the entire goal itself may not be worthy of the collective resources allotted to it. In any case, examining the root cause of delay or failure should help determine if the idea is salvageable.

In the church, the message never changes, but the methods can be updated to fit a more relevant approach to modern society. For example, there is nothing wrong with songbooks, but in a technological society, projecting the words on the screen seems to be more appealing and less cumbersome. Other examples could be cited that have to do more with tradition than with biblical mandate. It is a well-established fact that most people resist change. However, for the sake of efficiently moving the Gospel, changes can be beneficial. Many companies have failed over the years that have not faced the realities of their changing circumstances.

One of the most prolific business researchers of the 21st century related a story of the fate of two grocery giants in the last half of the 20th century (Collins, 2001). A leading grocery store in the 1900s was the Great Atlantic and Pacific Tea Company, commonly known as A & P. In 1959 this mammoth company celebrated 100 years of business and was one of the largest corporations in America. Another retail grocery store, Kroger, was much smaller and produced no dramatic returns for investors at that time. This began to change in the 1960s as

Kroger evolved to service a changing market while A & P insisted on traditional methods and services. The result was that in the last quarter of the 20th century, Kroger produced returns eighty times better than A & P. Finally, after 156 years, the failed giant ceased operations in November of 2015. The basis of A & P's demise was a failure to confront the realities of where the market was headed. Not facing the facts in an honest assessment ultimately closed the doors of one of the biggest business in American history.

A willingness to assess where the company was in light of changing market conditions could have preserved the giant and propelled it to new dimensions in the new millennium. Likewise, when we as Apostolic leaders fail to gauge the health of our goals and objectives, failure can ensue. Much worse than losing market share and upsetting shareholders, our failures have eternal consequences. In setting goals, let us remember that objective determination of progress is key in keeping the objectives on course.

Chapter Ten

Proper Communication

As leaders in some ministerial capacity, we do not traffic in goods or services. Rather, we are in the people business. This necessitates communication. In order to get things done, there needs to be exchange of information. Directives are given, plans formulated, ideas presented, feedback received, etc. Most of us have experienced, at one time or another, a breakdown in communication that produced disastrous results. It is incumbent upon leaders to hone the fine art of communication as much as possible.

The problem is that not everyone communicates in the same way. We all have different backgrounds, perceptions, biases, etc. that present challenges in how messages are conveyed and received. This dilemma is exacerbated in our modern era with the myriad types of communication devices. Previously we could judge, with relative certainty, the motive or spirit of a message simply by tone of voice. Not so anymore. Now we can receive texts, emails or other electronic messages and wonder what was meant by it. How many people have been offended by a message that was sent with no ill intent? For the leader, this predicament translates to a need for careful consideration of our words.

There are countless examples of messages being misconstrued or misinterpreted throughout history. Wars have been fought and conflicts escalated due to miscommunication. In November of 1956, Russian Premier Nikita Khrushchev addressed a group of Western ambassadors in Moscow. The infamous address has been scrutinized countless times as a famed threat to democracy in Khrushchev's declaration, "we will bury you." This was considered a shot heard around the world that heightened the emerging Cold War and fear of the spread of Communism. While it is unlikely the comment was intended to be anything less than antagonistic, when the whole quote is considered it can carry a bit of a different connotation. The context includes, "About capitalist states, it doesn't depend on you whether we [Soviet Union] exist. If you don't like us, don't accept our invitations, and don't invite us to come to see you. Whether you like it or not, history is on our side. We will bury you." Many historians have concluded that a more literal translation would carry the connotation that we will *attend* your funeral rather than we will *cause* your funeral. That's a rather significant difference.

In our leading in ministry, we need to choose our words wisely. We are not just delivering cargo that can be handled carelessly. Rather, we are handling the most precious commodity of all: the souls of men. While a bit of qualification may be in order, such as the idea that people need to be more thick-skinned or some such, the reality is that various factors interplay in the individual's life that affect how messages are received. I agree that walking on eggshells in order not to offend is typically not the best course of action. However, neither is a caustic approach in which consideration is disregarded as we impetuously rant with no semblance of rationality or respect. There needs to be a happy medium in which our point is made in a way that is least likely to be misinterpreted and most likely to be received correctly.

To empower and equip our teams, we need to be effective communicators. This is, of course, a key to building relationships, which is a key in leadership. What is the easiest way to build a solid relationship? It could be argued that simply talking is the most effective way. How we communicate is of the utmost importance. Most people would probably agree that the best approach is with old-fashioned kindness and sincerity. A respectful demeanor inherently gives a degree of credibility to the leader. Those we are leading are less likely to suspect ulterior motives or raise walls of resistance when approached with genuine concern for their ideas and wellbeing.

Biblical principles and examples could be cited to strengthen this idea. One negative example is found in I Samuel chapter 25. This is the story of David's request for minimal provision from Nabal in retribution for David's men protecting all that Nabal had. Per the testimony of those protected, David was, "a wall unto us both by night and day" (verse 16). Rather than offering the slightest token of gratitude for unrequested kindness and protection, Nabal railed on David's men ridiculing their request. When the righteous Abigail intervened to avert the impending tragedy of a just response, the crux of Nabal's issue was revealed. In making her plea to David, Abigail stated that her husband was, "such a son of Belial that a man cannot speak to him" (verse 17). Let it never be said of us that we cannot even be spoken to without fear of an unprovoked negative reaction.

In light of this story we find that another important component of effective leadership is being approachable. How many good ideas have not been offered for fear of irrational rejection? When we create an atmosphere in which people feel comfortable approaching us with thoughts or suggestions, it fosters creativity and openness. Such an environment has a propensity to maximize collective potential often either offering viable solutions to problems or even avoiding potential difficulties.

We could probably all cite leaders in the past who have possessed a Nabal type of approachability. Unfortunately, due to many factors such as ego, territorialism or some such irrational fear or dysfunction, such leaders can be prevalent in secular environments. By the grace of God may they be rarely found in Apostolic leaders. I personally have worked for a leader in the past who liked to posture as approachable with an open-door policy. However, in reality, when he was approached, the typical response was one of incredulity or suspicion. At times, his reaction was even demeaning. It didn't take long for subordinates to realize that the talk of an open-door policy welcoming healthy exchange of ideas was merely talk. This leader's credibility was soon diminished to the point of irrelevance as underlings chose to avoid unnecessary interaction with him opting rather to seek counsel elsewhere.

Perhaps the most damaging of the poor leader's habits was the propensity for impatience or even anger in response to reasonable requests.

This points to another integral component of effective leadership, namely the ability to control one's spirit. To put it plainly, moodiness and uncontrolled tempers have no place in church leadership. The Bible has much to say on this topic, which leaders would do well to consider. The wise man observed, "He that is slow to anger is better than the mighty; and he that ruleth his spirit than he that taketh a city" (Proverbs 16:32). He further admonished, "He that hath no rule over his own spirit is like a city that is broken down, and without walls" (Proverbs 25:28). The consequences of this demeanor are worthy of consideration.

The ideas expressed in the preceding verses are twofold. First, being slow to anger is more powerful than possessing the military fortitude to conquer. The reason is because such a one has conquered a much more formidable opponent: self. Taking a city requires being able to overpower and outmaneuver an opposing external force. However, ruling one's spirit requires conquering a commanding internal force. Secondly, having no rule over one's spirit is likened to a city without walls in that such a one is essentially defenseless. We open ourselves up to unmitigated attacks when we do not control our emotions.

Walled cities were often seen as impenetrable in the Old Testament. This is why the victory at Jericho was so miraculous. According to archeological excavation, the walls of Jericho were actually a series of walls totaling over 45 feet in height (A History of Israel, 2017). When the walls were broken down, the once impermeable city was relegated to an easily accessed and conquered village. Likewise, when we are not able to rule our own spirit, antagonistic forces can easily penetrate and wreak havoc on our influence as leaders.

Admittedly, ruling one's spirit can be a daunting task for some. This can be the case particularly when situations involve potentially high stakes and volatile emotions. The reality is that when emotion goes up, cognition goes down. This has been proven physiologically. When we feel threatened, chemicals are released that divert blood from our brains to our muscles. It is our body's way of preparing us for physical confrontation. The underlying effect is that the redirecting of this blood lowers our ability to reason. This is why people do not think straight when they are mad.

Consequently, it is wise to avoid decisions in the heat of the moment. It is much easier to make a rash decision that might be regretted when operating purely on emotion rather than careful consideration.

Besides the physiological aspect, a spiritual component certainly exists. Uncontrolled anger leaves one vulnerable to similar spirits. Jesus said that to be angry with our brother without a cause puts us in danger of the judgment (Matthew 5:22). The reason for this is that an emotional state of anger can escalate to physical altercation and even murder. In the same context, Jesus equates lusting after a woman with adultery. The principle is that the spirit behind the emotional drive is indistinguishable to the spirit behind the actual act. Therefore, to take heed to one's spirit is of paramount concern.

A plethora of Scripture further substantiates this principle. James 1:20 declares, "The wrath of man worketh not the righteousness of God." In other words, it is not possible to operate in the righteous realm the Lord requires while simultaneously yielding to fleshly temptations. Furthermore, Paul admonished to, "Be angry and sin not" (Ephesians 4:26). This shows that anger is not the primary culprit. Rather, it is our response to anger that is to be consciously calculated.

When we learn to channel that anger appropriately, our leadership ability is greatly enhanced.

Chapter Eleven

Self-Development

As Apostolic leaders in the 21st century, there are many things to consider. As we strive to develop the best course of action in our ministries, we can have a tendency to focus primarily outward. There must also be an inward reflection to get a fuller picture what is needed to be successful. There has to be an ongoing self-assessment to ensure our growth is commensurate with our goals. As church leaders, the ultimate measure of success is found in the accomplishing of our two primary goals, which are the salvation of the lost and the perfecting of the saints. If sinners are responding to the Gospel by repenting and being baptized in the name of Jesus and receiving the Holy Ghost, the ultimate goal of evangelism is being met. Likewise, if the saints are being strengthened, the goal of keeping people saved is being achieved.

However, we also need personal goals. As leaders we need to strive for self-improvement. No one living today has ever yet fully reached his or her potential. There are always more mountains to climb and enemies to conquer, even within ourselves. Striving to improve ourselves produces residual results with potentially far-reaching effects. When we examine ourselves as objectively as possible, we become aware of areas of strengths and weaknesses. Self-assessment is the first step to self-improvement. If we are unaware of areas in need of adjustment, we are not going to take the steps to better ourselves.

In our busy lives, it is easy to justify not taking time for personal development. The temptation is to comfort ourselves in knowing that our current abilities and knowledge have gotten us to where we are. The next logical assumption is that these skills are adequate for greater accomplishments. After all, it is the anointing that makes all the difference, and we are just pawns fulfilling the wishes of the master. Such thinking is flawed on many levels. First, while the anointing is certainly the primary element in any Apostolic ministry (see chapter 3), God does expect us to participate in the process. This is why the angel did not preach the plan of salvation to Cornelius in Acts chapter 10. Rather, Cornelius was instructed to call for Peter who would, "tell thee what thou oughtest to do" (Acts 10:6). Peter had to be responsive to the call of God in order for salvation to be offered to the Gentiles.

Another problem with believing our current skill level is sufficient for greater achievements is the fact that we live in an ever-evolving world. The problems that plagued the church just 10 or 20 years ago are not the same issues of today. With every generation and every technological advance, it seems there are new concerns to combat. These often require current knowledge to even know the basics of an issue.

Of course there are timeless considerations that must be at the forefront of the leader's mind. I have taught a graduate course several times entitled "Current Issues in Pentecostal Ministry." While the class was true to its name in defining the topics as current issues, the reality was that many of them are actually ongoing issues that every generation has to grapple with. One is fidelity and resisting temptation. As a required text, we used a compelling novel by Francine Rivers entitled *And the Shofar Blew*. The real-life story depicted a pastor whose life became unbalanced as he relentlessly pursued ministry goals to the neglect and detriment of key relationships. Moral failure ensued until he finally received a personal awakening before it was too late. This convincingly depicted the danger of neglecting personal devotion.

The first area of concern is indeed personal devotion and spirituality. As leaders in an Apostolic church, our primary focus is not on skills or talents, but rather on our personal spiritual life. Are we praying consistently? Are we students of the Word of God? Are we practitioners of spiritual disciplines necessary for personal spirituality? This effort requires consistent diligence as increasing demands and fleshly tendencies war against our efforts to remain spiritually minded.

As foundational as spirituality is, there is much more involved in developing ourselves to be effective leaders. We are holistic beings and therefore are not able to maximize our effectiveness by focusing exclusively on one area. We are body, soul and spirit (I Thessalonians 5:23). We are also commanded to love the Lord with all of our heart, soul and might (Deuteronomy 6:5). This encompasses every part of us and implies that our service is inadequate if one of these elements is lacking. To serve the Lord with our heart, or center of emotions, but not with our mind, limits our ability to minister.

The Lord has gifted each one of us with the ability to learn and increase knowledge. Few things are more worthy of our time than reading practical books and articles that provide insights into leadership practices. Thankfully, there are many more books by Apostolic authors than there were just a few years ago. With the increase in technology and greater access to information, Apostolic authors are rising who are willing to share practical tips for leading God's people. Many of these are pastors who possess a wealth of wisdom gained through decades of experience. Others are lay ministers who have studied to show themselves approved and have gained theoretical knowledge along with practical experience. There are also many websites that are dedicated to Apostolic leadership. Committing just a few hours a week to the pursuit of knowledge readily available can exponentially increase our understanding of leadership concepts.

Self-development can also involve taking classes that pertain to our ministry. In the past, such a proposition could be justifiably avoided due to the time constraints involved in driving to and from a campus and being required to be present at a particular time. Today there are online options that conveniently allow leaders to glean knowledge and interact with other leaders. The synergistic effect of such collaboration is staggering. I personally have had the honor of interacting with great Apostolic men of God in online classes as both a student and instructor over the past several years. I have heard countless testimonies of how these classes have revolutionized their churches. Some of the pastors I studied with built new churches within a year or two of completing their programs. This is neither to say that a degree necessitates growth, nor that these men would not have experienced revival without this element. However, their own testimonies attribute the dramatic change in their thinking that was perpetuated through their involvement in studying with like-minded pastors.

The Scripture teaches, "Iron sharpeneth iron; so a man sharpeneth the countenance of his friend" (Proverbs 27:17). Fellowshipping with the people of God who are committed to common goals can be a vital part of personal development. Like other aspects of becoming the best you, this often involves deliberate actions. In our busy society, it is unlikely that we are going to run into other Apostolic leaders casually throughout our day. Instead, we often need to schedule time for fellowship and connecting. This does not have to be a formal affair, but can be over lunch or another casual setting. For pastors, this could involve inviting ministers to preach for them. Connecting may not always be convenient, but there is strength gained through intentional scheduling of fellowship.

Chapter Twelve

Developing Others

The most obvious effect of leadership is observable results. When the job is being accomplished as planned, the leader is hailed as the driving force behind the success. Likewise, when the efforts are failing, the focus is on what the leader is doing wrong. This is certainly a natural way of viewing and judging leaders. In the secular world, such assessments determine whether leaders keep their jobs, get promotions, or get reassigned. In the Kingdom of God, visible results are also reflected on the leader. The pastor of a church that has 20 members after 25 years is likely to be considered a poor leader. It is entirely possible that circumstances unbeknownst to most people could have contributed to the church's woes and the leader's ineffectiveness. However, the fact that essentially no growth has occurred after a considerable amount of time creates a consensus of negative opinion. While it can be scripturally proven that bearing fruit should always be the result of Apostolic ministry, there is a possibility that the leader in a situation like this could have produced more inconspicuous results.

One such accomplishment could be the development of leaders within the church. While this may not be hailed as a grand achievement, in reality the compounded effect can exceed readily observable results. Incumbent upon Apostolic leaders is the nurturing and development of others. A leading Apostolic church in America has a nesting vision, "Helping people become." What this translates to is creating an environment in which anyone can catch the vison of developing into something that he or she desires to be. The culture of such a church is one of endless possibilities and faith. This conviction is rooted in the fact that with God all things are possible. This coupled with the reality that we are made in the image of God and called to be His ambassadors in the Earth creates a boldness to step into uncharted territory.

Some who are timid and content to settle for much less than God desires for them begin to receive a revelation of possibility. Perhaps generational strongholds have kept their family locked into a mentality of minimal opportunity. When exposed to great leadership, faith and confidence rise as potential is unleashed. In order to begin this journey to greatness, leaders need to intentionally cultivate an environment of faith and opportunity.

As leaders, it is much easier to create followers than develop leaders. When we delegate tasks and timelines, we create followers. When we delegate authority and accountability, we create leaders (Bentley, 2018). It is more natural, and admittedly easier, to do the former. This is particularly the case when the greatest emphasis is placed on accomplishing the task. When leaders realize that achieving the immediate objective is only part of the picture, they can structure the undertaking in a way that produces two-fold results. Not only is the current task completed, but it is done so in a way that fosters the development of others.

A common phrase is, "If you want something done right, do it yourself." Imagine if this thinking were reframed to be, "If you want someone to develop, don't worry if they do it wrong." Making mistakes is a necessary part of the process of development. This takes patience on both the part of the leader and the one who is developing. Think of a mother planting a garden with her child by her side. It is obviously much easier for the mom to do all the work while the child observes. There is a temptation to take this easy way out to simply get the seeds planted and move on. However, a wise mother will seize the opportunity to allow the child to till up the soil, drop in the seed and cover the seed with dirt. Then she allows the child to water the seed and check on it daily. Being involved in the process teaches much more than mere observation can. Allowing the child to get his hands dirty will personalize the experience and cause it to sink deeper into his psyche. He will not only feel accomplished (even if he did not do things perfectly), but he will also gain a physical connection with elements involved.

Leading saints in Apostolic ministry is much like the scenario described above. People must be given the opportunity to be involved in the administration of the ministry. Allowing those we are developing to formulate plans, enlist helpers and coordinate activities creates a sense of ownership. Furthermore, when these developing leaders are given the liberty to problem solve, they gain greater understanding of another level of leadership. This is particularly the case when the problems they are solving were in part created by their own miscalculations. Nothing teaches problem solving quite like cleaning up self-made messes.

The natural question to ask ourselves when we embark on the process of developing others is, "Where do I start?" To be effective in creating leaders who will support the mission of the church and who will personally grow to be autonomous, there needs to be an understanding of where each person initially stands. As individuals, each one possesses unique skills and experiences that have either helped prepare them for leadership or have created inhibitors for effective leadership. Leaders are not developed overnight, neither do they develop at the same pace. Some need general direction and minimal authority to develop leadership skills through practical exercise. Others need more specific examples and directions as they gingerly experiment with leadership responsibilities. One key to developing leaders appropriately is understanding where they are on the continuum. There is a danger in attempting to expedite the process beyond the current ability or desire of a developing leader. Determining appropriate action for individuals being developed will help eliminate frustration for all involved.

Investing in the development of people in our churches involves a bit of vulnerability. We can never truly be effective in creating leaders if we insist on holding their hand at all times. Neither can we expect desired results if our approach is to give them a manual of sorts and expect them to figure it out. At the heart of our approach must be faith and trust. In other words, we need to believe in those we are mentoring. We must believe that their desire is to do right and to expand the kingdom. Naturally, there will be some whose ulterior motives might be more self-serving, but generally we need to approach our task by believing in them. We also must appreciate their willingness to move to another level. For some, moving out of an area of comfort is a scary proposition. Reaching for new heights might be something they have avoided due to fear or lack of confidence. Their willingness to better themselves while propagating the Gospel deserves our celebration and appreciation.

Throughout the process of developing leaders, we need to be quick to rejoice in their victories. We also need to show patience and understanding when inevitable mistakes occur. Teachable moments will abound as fledgling leaders progress through the stages of development. It is never wise to punish people for mistakes. Rather, the approach needs to be one of evaluating what when wrong. The question is not, "Who is to blame?" but rather, "Where do we go from here?" Then we can make an informed assessment of the best course of action moving forward. Some mistakes are more costly than others. For example, miscalculating the amount of food needed for a fellowship dinner carries far less consequence than a personnel faux pas that offends a brother and causes him to withdraw from the church. In either scenario, there is an opportunity to teach leadership skills.

One thing to keep in mind when embarking on the development of others is the fact that people are often a product of their environment. We see this in every walk of life. The pervasive mindset of those we surround ourselves with undoubtedly affects our mentality. You have probably encountered some with a poverty mentality. Their whole outlook on life is that they will always be stuck where they are with zero opportunity for upward mobility. By contrast, there are those who seem to be born with a winning attitude that says, "I can do anything and nothing can stop me." Our job as leaders is to break the poverty mentality and instill a mentality of success. To do so requires creating a climate conducive to leadership. The importance of positivity in this environment cannot be overemphasized.

Incumbent upon leaders is the responsibility to not only gauge the current mindset of developing leaders, but to also effect change in this climate. One leadership expert observed that leaders must be more like thermostats than thermometers (Maxwell, 1997). This is a profound revelation as it shows that simply being aware of current conditions is not enough. Rather, we need the ability to change the atmosphere through our words and actions. This requires intentional interaction with those we are mentoring. When a leader creates an atmosphere conducive to success, bringing others into the fold becomes a much easier proposition.

Many elements need to coalesce for a sustainable climate of leadership to exist. An example from nature could be a flower. For a flower to grow, many things need to be present. There has to be rich soil, moisture and sunshine. If one of these becomes compromised, the growth likewise becomes inhibited. Likewise, if too much of any of these elements is present, the natural progress will be stymied. Ideal development requires ideal conditions. Of course, we are not plants and do possess much more aptitude for resilience. Nevertheless, the principle remains the same. The more we can invest into creating a positive climate for leadership, the greater the likelihood of leaders being developed. This is why constantly monitoring the atmosphere is crucial. For example, if complaining and discontentment become pervasive, the malcontents involved can quickly infect the environment. An observant leader will recognize dangerous conditions in the atmosphere and intervene accordingly.

In assessing leadership potential, key factors can be observed. Arguably the most important of these is attitude. Someone whose focus is continually negative would present a much bigger challenge to development than one who emphasizes the positive aspects of a situation. There are those who would complain if they won one million dollars because they had to pay taxes. There are others whose undeserved calamities have not elicited a cynical or negative attitude, but rather have contributed to resiliency and thankfulness for what has gone well. This is not to say that the former group could never contain future leaders. Rather, the point is that possessing a positive attitude gives a considerable advantage to one aspiring to leadership.

Other factors that need to be present to identify a likely candidate for leadership include loyalty, discipline and, of course, integrity. Each of these could warrant a chapter by itself. For our purposes, let's briefly identify key sub factors of these attributes. The first one to consider is loyalty.

Does the potential leader have a readily identifiable history with the church? This is not necessarily referring entirely to the time he or she has been in church, although this also should be considered before giving too much responsibility. The bigger question is, has this person shown commitment to the greater cause of the Kingdom? Is he or she "sold out" and obviously interested in doing everything possible to see the work of God move forward? Whether one has been in church for six months or 20 years, it does not take a long observation to see if he or she possesses loyalty to the cause. Also worthy of consideration is how personally committed such a potential leader is to their local church. Are there signs that he or she is just passing through or hanging around for exclusively personal benefit? Those who demonstrate these tendencies are less than ideal candidates for leadership development.

Discipline is another necessary trait for potential leaders. This is similar to faithfulness, which is discussed in another chapter, but carries a somewhat different connotation. Discipline equates to a commitment to do what is needed even at inconvenient times. A disciplined person does not avoid responsibility due to less than ideal circumstances. Rather, he or she fulfills duties reliably. Such a person understands the value of the work being done and recognizes the importance of his or her role. An undisciplined person, by contrast, fulfils tasks in an obligatory manner, but only if current circumstances warrant participation. For these people, there is little regard for the overall health of the organization. The most important consideration is personal preference and comfort.

Integrity must also be present in anyone who desires to develop as a leader. This is integral in any organization and is magnified in a church setting. Unscrupulous people with self-serving ambitions are not good candidates for leadership development. They might be effective in more menial tasks, but entrusting them with the responsibility of leadership is a formula for disaster. Any potential leader needs to be trustworthy and honest. Their character needs to be communicated through words and actions. Identifying the congruence of these two takes more than casual observation. Instead, this involves spending time with potential leaders and possibly even with their families. No one knows us better than our families.

In Apostolic leaders, there needs to be a willingness to introduce those we are developing to new realities. One area that is often lacking in Apostolic circles is exposure. Many precious saints and potential leaders are simply unaware of the possibilities that exist. Leaders who are serious about producing other leaders do not fear the effect of exposing them to the realm of endless possibility. This can come in many forms. There is a plethora of leadership material available that can enhance one's understanding of basic principles of leadership. Also, there are examples of greatness all around us, particularly in Apostolic churches. Sadly, some leaders do not want to expose saints to those who have been successful due to imagined fears. One trick of the enemy is to convince unwitting pastors that allowing saints to observe or interact with successful pastors would illicit a desire to leave their church to connect with something bigger and better. The reality is that exposing potential leaders to successful pastors and ministers will enlighten them to the possibility of greatness in their own congregation.

One effective way to expose potential leaders to the inner workings of successful churches is to visit some of those churches. The best venue for this is typically visiting during a conference. Many powerful Apostolic conferences exist that can introduce developing leaders to greatness in Apostolic circles. While there can be travel and expense involved, this is a worthy investment. It may not be possible or practical to attend several conferences across the United States to gain a breadth of knowledge in a short period of time. However, depending on where one's church is located, there is likely a dynamic conference within a day's drive. Even taking one or two potential leaders with you to a conference can expedite the process of leadership development. If possible, a pastor could repeat this two or three times a year and expose several leaders to examples of world-class leadership. He then could follow up after the event with a debriefing for those who attended as well as others who were not able to attend.

As mentioned, there is no shortage of leadership books, videos, websites and other materials available today. These provide cost-effective ways for leadership development. An Apostolic leader who is developing other leaders could assign books to read or videos to watch and then follow up with a leadership meeting to discuss principles presented. This not only gives valuable insight of these principles to developing leaders; it also cultivates an atmosphere of leadership development. This can create a thirst among those in attendance as well as in other aspiring leaders. The realization that the Lord desires to use each one of us to expand the Kingdom of God can provide a motivating impetus for development.

Growth opportunities such as those mentioned above also provide ongoing motivation which is necessary for continued development. Always striving to improve ensures that stagnation will not occur. A key understanding that needs to be communicated to developing leaders is that there is always more to learn. There is always the possibility of greater effectiveness. While it may be tempting to bask in accomplishments instead of reaching for more, the reality is that there is always more to be done. Until the last sinner prays through, our work is not done. There will always be a need for developing leaders.

Chapter Thirteen

Balance

There are several reasons why leaders might step down from, or become frustrated in, a leadership position. Primary reasons are often fatigue and burnout. Simply put, they run out of steam and lose their motivation. This can be attributed to overworking, not properly utilizing resources or being focused to the point of neglecting other important responsibilities. At some point, the leader who experiences these things has gotten out of balance. We are not designed to move constantly without taking a break. Even in creation, the Lord rested on the seventh day. This is not because He was tired, but rather to set an example for us. Working around the clock with no personal time often results in several negative consequences.

One thing that usually suffers in these cases is relationships. When an individual is focused entirely on the mission, no matter how honorable and necessary it may be, those closest to this person can feel neglected or second-rate. This phenomenon is not exclusive to pastors. Other ministers can experience the same thing. In fact, this can be observed in many areas of life, including business. One example involves a contractor in the Midwest with whom I was acquainted previously. His story illustrates the need for balance.

This savvy business owner's drive for success in his concrete company was so strong that it consumed him. He would work 80 or 90 hours a week in building a large, successful business. He constantly sought to increase his knowledge, train his employees and outmaneuver the competition. His was initially a relatively small company taking on behemoth, union-backed enterprises. Within a few short years, he was a leading competitor and had built a multi-million dollar company. He became renowned in the area and even accepted speaking engagements around the country. His corporate success was undeniable. Sadly, however, his home life did not enjoy the same level of prosperity. During the course of building his enterprise, his wife divorced him. His relationships with his children suffered as well. What should have taken precedence in his life was neglected to the point of destruction.

Such collateral damage is not acceptable in the church. As Apostolic leaders, our primary responsibility must be to our families. We are called to lead them first. If this responsibility is not met, our overall effectiveness will suffer. To meet the needs of our family, we must be intentional in consistently carving out time for them. The reality is that we could be busy at every moment and still feel like we not accomplishing everything that needs to be done. Rather than frustrating ourselves and those we love, we must consciously strive to spend quality time strengthening these relationships.

Creating balance in our life and ministry does not necessarily translate to giving equal time to each activity. We do not have to be so compartmentalized as to cease operations in one area because we hit the time allotted for the week. Rather, a good approach is to assess the responsibilities of the week and map out a strategy to accomplish goals. For example, if someone knows ten hours is needed for a certain task, it is wise to set a tentative schedule for completion. This might consist of allotting two hours a day or perhaps a full day. The point is that focusing too much on ministry without regard to other necessary duties will cause inefficiency and frustration. Some ministers even set "appointments" with their family to ensure that they do not become consumed with other responsibilities. Without proper planning, the likelihood of becoming unbalanced increases significantly.

Being cognizant of certain potential pitfalls can assist us in maintaining balance. One of these, which is very easy to become ensnared by, is overcommitting. It is honorable to have a desire to help out wherever needed. As leaders, our natural tendency is to be doers and to engage in as many ways as possible to expand the Kingdom of God. This can present a danger if we are afraid to say no. Perhaps you have heard of the rule of 80/20. It has been reported, if not scientifically observed, that 20% of the people in a church do 80% of the work. The assumption is that if you are reading this book, you are likely part of the 20%. Your desire to contribute in multiple ways is not a bad thing. Desire is a key ingredient in effectiveness. The danger can occur when you fail to calculate how much you can actually commit to doing.

To remain balanced, one must not excessively allocate resources to one particular responsibility. Again, this does not mean that for every hour spent working, one hour must be spent relaxing. As euphoric as this sounds, it is not realistic. We do not require an amount of rest equal to our amount of work. What it does mean is that we must recognize that our time and ability to contribute is limited. This makes the efficient use of our time even more necessary. Of all the commodities we can access, time is the least renewable.

Overcommitting essentially amounts to saying yes to too many things. Prioritization is key in determining how much we should commit. Questions we should ask ourselves are, "Will this new commitment detract from my effectiveness in current obligations?" or "Will this opportunity negatively impact important relationships due to the time involved?" It is better to turn down an opportunity than to agree to more than we can handle.

Over commitment can also have spiritual repercussions. When we are squeezed for time, there is a temptation to neglect our daily devotion. Inordinate focus on objectives can taint our understanding of the value of personal consecration. This is one reason why overly busy leaders sometimes fall into moral failure. If we are too busy to pray, we are definitely out of balance and need to step back and reassess. The difficultly in this is that those who are in this state usually do not realize it. Being intensely focused on tasks can shield us from the realization that we are neglecting our personal spiritual lives. Much like Martha in Luke chapter 10, we can be "cumbered about much serving" and view Mary's devotion as laziness. In this passage, the Lord did not rebuke Martha for her attentiveness to responsibility, but rather highlighted that Mary's choice of sitting at His feet was much more productive.

So it is in our lives as leaders. The Lord is not displeased that we are dedicated to being about our Father's business. Jesus instructed His disciples to pray that the Lord of the harvest would send forth laborers into the harvest (Matthew 9:38). More important is "that good part" which Mary chose. Service without relationship is obligatory routine. Service accompanied with relationship is fulfilling and gratifying ministry.

There are practical ways to combat our propensity to be unaware of our spiritual deficiencies. One such way is through relationships of accountability. If you are married, the best choice for this role is your spouse. A man must allow his wife to offer observations as to her assessment of his devotional habits. This could potentially be a precarious situation if a wife looked at it as an opportunity to point out every fault. This is not the goal of this scenario. Rather, since a husband and wife are more intimately connected than any other relationship, observation of spiritual disciplines should be natural. This can be mutually beneficial as helping each other spiritually will have a positive effect on other relationships.

Another consideration is to have close friends or mentors connect with you frequently to gauge your overall health and balance. Some things are noticeable by physical observation. For example, if you were neglecting sleep, it is likely that a weekly check-in with an accountability partner would alert him to this. Our appearance can reveal deficiencies of which we are not aware.

Beyond the apparent concerns, meetings such as this can provide a venue for trusted confidantes to ask difficult questions. He or she might probe into areas of your life that are not immediately apparent. They might ask if you have been praying every day, or if you have missed any church services that week. They might also inquire as to any concerns your spouse may have voiced. It is easy to disregard observations from your wife and to dismiss them as inaccurate perceptions or a lack of understanding. Meeting with a third party might give more validity to these concerns as this can allow a deeper discussion.

In order to maintain balance in our lives there also has to be time for disconnecting from the day to day. This can be accomplished by going on vacation or even just getting away for a weekend. Depending on your location, there may be tranquil areas perfectly suited for relaxation. A couple of days in the mountains or by a body of water can clear our minds and refresh our energy. The more one can disconnect from pressing demands, the more effective the retreat can be. It may not be possible or practical to leave your phone for a day or two. If not, a good approach is to leave it in the room while you go for a walk or sit on the beach. It will be there when you get back and being away from it can help you relax more freely.

Getting away for days at a time might seem like a luxury afforded to few. Even if this is not possible, you might consider a day trip to a remote area or even a drive in the country. The time and expense involved is not the primary consideration. Rather, the goal is to force yourself to take a break and allow for down time.

Another strategy to avoid being overcommitted and out of balance is to learn the art of delegation. Some leaders feel that they must personally do everything or at least oversee everything that is to be done. While this may be the case when the ministry is small, the goal is for ministries to grow. At some point, a single leader will not be able to handle everything in the department or church. If this point is never reached, then leadership has failed to produce intended results.

The idea of delegation ties back to that of developing others. A goal of Apostolic leaders is to produce other leaders who will be able to shoulder the load. These emerging leaders are invaluable as we try to do business in deep waters. In order to utilize these willing vessels effectively, we need to be willing to release responsibility to them. This is usually done incrementally. Part of our job as leaders is to assess the competency, loyalty and willingness of those we lead. Do they seem passionate about the work being done? Are they more interested in self-advancement or personal gain than in accomplishing the goals of the ministry? Are they responsive to direction or argumentative? Assessments like these help determine if one is capable of having tasks delegated to their care.

Another thing to keep in mind when delegating is to convey expectations clearly. If someone fails in an assigned task, a good question to ask ourselves is whether the directive was easy to understand. Just because we know exactly what needs to be done and how it should be done does not mean that others possess the same understanding. This is where patience as a leader becomes important. If we are upset with someone for not executing assigned duties appropriately, it is imperative that we do not show that frustration. Belittling or excoriating someone for making a mistake does not build trust. Rather, such a reaction can have a counter effect of alienation and retreat. The next time we need something done, one who was chastised for failure will be unlikely to volunteer again.

One powerful benefit of delegation is the ability to accomplish much more than we could on our own. A basic concept that many are familiar with is that of synergy. Simply put, collaborating our efforts produces greater results than individual efforts combined. What this means is that two people working together on a project can accomplish more than two working individually. This is naturally compounded when a team is utilized. Several people who are unified and working toward a common goal can produce sustainable results. In Genesis chapter 11 we find that even rebellious people, when unified, can create a formidable force. The Lord looked down from Heaven and observed those building the Tower of Babel and declared, "Behold, the people is one, and they have all one language; and this they begin to do: and now nothing will be restrained from them, which they have imagined to do" (Genesis 11:6).

Observable concepts from this passage are noteworthy. First, the Lord is the one who made the observation. What God declares is not opinion, but absolute truth. The unity of these rebels was so strong that they would have accomplished any task unless the Lord intervened otherwise. Secondly, God said they all had one language. We know that this is the origin of languages in which the Lord confused the tongues to thwart the attempted coup. There is a deeper meaning as well. They were speaking the same language in unity of purpose. Evidently no one was murmuring about the order of operations. No one wanted to usurp Nimrod's leadership in the construction project. No one was complaining about the hours or pay. Intense focus was the order of the day.

Since having one language is necessary for maximum efficiency, it makes one wonder if this is why the children of Israel were commanded to stay silent as they marched around Jericho. The explicit command from Joshua was, "Ye shall not shout, nor make any noise with your voice, neither shall any word proceed out of your mouth" (Joshua 6:10). In other words, shut up and march. Few things can sabotage unity quicker than negative talk. Diligently combatting this must be priority for every leader. When followers are unified in purpose, delegation can be profitable. When delegation is profitable, balance is more attainable for the leader.

Final Thoughts

It is my desire that this book has enhanced your understanding of key elements of Apostolic leadership. The information contained does not propose to be comprehensive. There are a host of other considerations for those striving to minister in this modern arena.

While any number of resources available can assist in developing leadership skills, the goal of this project was to highlight areas necessary for effective Apostolic leadership. Along with the challenges every leader faces, those who lead God's people face the added element of spiritual realities, both positive and negative.

Some elements are beyond our control and therefore unavoidable. However, those described herein represent areas of which we have been granted stewardship. We can practice faithfulness, earnestly seek the Lord for the anointing, choose how we respond to conflict, etc.

It is also incumbent upon us as leaders to develop ourselves and others and to learn how to most effectively communicate with fellow laborers. Among the greatest of our responsibilities is striving for balance to keep our ministries fresh and our vital relationships healthy.

References

Bentley, Andrew. "A Discussion on Coaching." Interview by
    author. March 6, 2019.

Bentley, Andrew. "Principles of Succession." *Instagram*,
    October 7, 2018,
    https://www.instagram.com/bentley238/.

Brock, Annie, and Heather Hundley. *The Growth Mindset*.
    Berkeley, CA: Ulysses Press, 2016.

Bryant, Adam. "Google's Quest to Build a Better Boss." The
    New York Times. March 12, 2011.
    https://www.nytimes.com/2011/03/13/usiness/13hire.ht
    ml?pagewanted=1&_r=1.

Collins, Jim. *Good to Great*. New York, NY: HarperCollins,
    2001.

Maxwell, John C. *The 360 Degree Leader*. Nashville, TN:
    Thomas Nelson, 2005.

Maxwell, John C. *Becoming a Person of Influence*. Nashville,
    TN: Thomas Nelson, 199

Phillips, Donald T. *Lincoln on Leadership*. New York, NY:
    Business Plus, 1992.

"Principles of Peacekeeping." United Nations. 2019.
https://peacekeeping.un.org/en/principles-of-
peacekeeping.

"The Walls of Jericho." A History of Israel. 2017.
http://www.israel-a-history-of.com/walls-of-
jericho.html.

To contact the author for services or leadership seminars, please email ddeanderson@yahoo.com